Grow and Develop People... "The Old Guy"

LITTLE LEADERSHIP LESSONS

...

FROM AN OLD GUY

VOLUME 02

by GLENN VAN EKEREN

Copyright 2021 by Glenn Van Ekeren.
All rights reserved.

No part of this book may be used or reproduced in any manner whatsoever without written permission from the author, except for the use of brief quotations in a book review.

Your support of the author's rights is appreciated.

Imprint: Independently published

For information regarding permission or distribution, contact **gvanekeren@vhs.com**

To discover more about the author visit **enthusedaboutlife.com**

ISBN: 978-1-7350962-1-6

A Word Of Thanks From The Old Guy

I'm so grateful for the countless people who have been an encouragement in my professional career.

Thank you to mentors who lovingly guided my path yet gave me the freedom to think, learn and grow on my own.

Thank you to professional colleagues whose passion for excellence challenged me to never settle for good enough.

Thank you to leaders who believed in me, encouraged me to stretch my expectations, and gave me the confidence to pursue my potential.

A special thank you to the team members I've been privileged to lead. You taught me the value of serving, caring and doing what's right for people.

One's career is rarely fulfilling without a family's unconditional acceptance and sometimes silent motivation that communicates; "You can do it!" Thank you family!

Initial Thoughts from the Old Guy...

Herb Kelleher was the founder and CEO of Southwest Airlines. When he died in 2019, the business world lost an icon, maverick and people focused leader in the industry. He was truly a people person.

Kelleher believed, "The business of business is people." He lived that philosophy in his daily actions as CEO. Southwest team members knew Herb Kelleher considered them Southwest Airline's number one asset. Every decision, conversation, or action Kelleher considered kept people's welfare at the top of the hierarchy.

There is nothing more important in an organization than people, and the privilege to lead people is certainly a premier calling.

Leaders possess the incredible opportunity to touch and transform people's lives. "The growth and development of people," wrote Dale Galloway, "is the highest calling of a leader." Our highest honor is to continually look for the best in people and instigate and nurture their growth.

One of my favorite scenes in the Academy Award-winning film As Good As It Gets is when Carol (portrayed by actress Helen Hunt) becomes so infuriated with Melvin (portrayed by actor Jack Nicholson) that she gets up from the restaurant table and is ready to leave. Melvin looks at her quizzically and quite stunned. He doesn't have a clue that he just insulted her with a flippant comment. He asks her to sit down; she obliges and responds, "Melvin, pay me a compliment. I need one and quick. You have no idea how much what you just said hurt my feelings."

Melvin is paralyzed. He mutters something and Carol lets him know that it's not even close to a compliment. She demands, "Now or never!" Melvin pauses for a moment, goes into a confusing description of his ailment and then ends his disjointed comments with: "You make me want to be a better man."

Shocked, Carol responds: "I think this is about the best compliment of my life."

People are grateful for leaders who help them grow, develop, blossom... become better people. That's why Herb Kelleher was such a popular, effective, results producing leader. Southwest team members always knew Kelleher had their future, best interests and personal and professional growth at the top of his priority list. Leaders inspire people to become a better version of themselves.

In my heart, I'm fervently convinced the number one priority for a leader is people.

The way we see people. The way we interact with people. The culture we build for people. The way we lead people.

And, our attitude about people's abilities, motivation and potential.

As Walt Disney said, "You can dream, create, design, and build the most wonderful place in the world. . . but it requires people to make the dream a reality."

Leaders have the privilege of looking for lives to change, hearts to encourage and minds to stimulate so they can make dreams a reality.

I hope these Little Leadership Lessons will plant you firmly on the path of creating a culture that makes an incredible difference in people's lives.

Become a Wizard

Reveal What Already Exists.

―――――――――

When my son was a senior in high school, he played the Tin Man in the high school version of "The Wizard of Oz." Through numerous rehearsals and performances, I became acutely aware that The Wizard of Oz was a leadership training program in disguise.

How is that you ask?

No doubt you remember how Dorothy was swept away in a tornado and is trying to find her way back to Kansas. Unfortunately, all the people around her are little Munchkins who have never heard of Kansas and have no interest in leaving their 'little' world. So, she's off to see the Wizard of Oz via the yellow brick road.

Along the way, Dorothy encounters a Tin Man wanting a heart and a Scarecrow professing to need a brain. Together they make their way into the forest petrified they will encounter the fearful "lions and tigers and bears, oh my! Lions and tigers and bears." And they did. The first creature they encounter is the one they fear the most. Ironically, the one they fear the most—the Lion—claims to be in dire need of some courage.

Each is convinced they must find their way to the Wizard who will fulfill their wishes and needs. This pitiful trio, lacking courage, brains, and heart, join Dorothy who lacks direction, and must overcome countless adversity to reach Oz. The wicked witch, flying monkeys and ugly castle guards nearly defeated them.

Alas, they arrived only to find the Wizard of Oz was a farce. A fake. A phony who hides behind a curtain. Yet, the Wizard is magical and convinces each of them they already possess what they are looking for.

The wizard looks the lion in the eye and says, "I know what your problem is, you don't have any medals. Here's a medal. Now you're brave, go out and act that way!" The lion's personal image was transformed. He believed the magical wizard.

Remember how the scarecrow believed he needed a brain. The wizard resolved that issue by issuing him a diploma and verbally announcing his intellect. Even the Tin Man believed the wizard when he gave him a clock that represented his beating heart. Impressive!

How about Dorothy? How does she get home to Kansas? She has certainly endured a tremendous struggle to find her answer. Remember, her journey was made wearing the ruby red slippers. She didn't understand their significance or how to use them. The Wizard changed all of that by telling her to concentrate with all of her might while saying the right words – "Voila! Kansas."

I'm old enough to remember the great song by the group America that included this line, "no Oz never did give nothing to the Tin Man that he didn't already have."

A phony wizard becomes a hero by revealing "what already exists." Leaders can perform that same, magical, heroic action by revealing the talents your team members already possess.

Dynamic leaders understand their primary responsibility is to transform talent into performance. Thomas J. Watson would have agreed with this strategy. He believed,

"The real difference between success and failure in a corporation can very often be traced to the question of how well the organization brings out the energies and talents of its people."

Questions to Ponder:

1. Perform an intentional talent inventory. How can I reveal to people the talents I discover in them?

Lessons in the Sand

The More Control You Use, the More Control You Lose.

Several years ago, our family took a winter vacation to Marco Island in Southwest Florida to visit my wife's parents. My mother-in-law suggested upon arrival that we should go shell hunting in the morning once the tide goes out.

"What time is that?" I asked.

She checked the local paper and informed me the tide would go out the next morning at 6:07 a.m. I wasn't exactly planning to go shell hunting at 6:00 a.m. in the morning while on vacation but I ultimately gave in to the idea.

As the waves slapped against my ankles in the shallow waters of the Gulf of Mexico, I began to feel a little motion sickness. I found myself a comfortable place to plop down on the beach's beautiful white sand and watched my family collect a precious haul of shells.

As I sat watching, I scooped up a handful of sand and closed my hand around it. This became a fascinating experiment. The tighter I clenched my fist the more sand slipped through the cracks of my fingers. When I gently held a clump of sand and shook my fist, hardly any sand was lost. The tighter the grip, the less sand I had. The lighter the grip, the more sand I could retain in my hand.

It's a paradox.

The more control a leader attempts to force on people, the more control they lose.

Passion fades, enthusiasm diminishes, commitment wavers, creativity suffers, and productivity is lost to 'slippage.'

Define the outcomes you want and then let each team member determine their path to making it happen. Give people control and responsibility for their processes. This can be messy, but it is the most productive way to get people focused on their performance.

I know it can be confusing and at times frustrating. A leader's apprehension about giving people freedom to do what they do was best expressed by New York Yankees owner George Steinbrenner. He was discussing his view on team ownership when he said, "I used to be very hands-on, but lately I've been more hands-off and I plan to become more hands-on and less hands off and hope that hands-on will become better than hands-off, the way hands-on used to be."

Confusing? No doubt!

Let's be clear. Set the standard. Get out of the way and let people go for it. Support wherever possible. Coach if necessary. Reward them for the results they produce. Reset the bar and do it all over again.

Hands off is better than hands on used to be . . . or something like that.

Questions to Ponder:
1. What's the 'grip pressure' I have on people?
2. How might I loosen up and give people the freedom to prove themselves?

Finding Their Reason

People Do Things For Their Reasons Not Your Reasons.

———————

"It is the greatest folly to talk of motivating anybody," said Patrick Emington. "The real key is to help others to unlock and direct their deepest motivators."

Here's a powerful question to ponder. What do my team members need right now? You might think this is an unreasonable expectation. Leaders often argue they supervise 15 or 20 people; so how in the world could they know what each person needs? Leadership is about personalization and individualization.

Lou Holtz suggested, "Everyone is special. Everyone has special needs and desires. The one trick is to find out what those needs are. Then if you treat people special, if you help them get what they want, you can't help but succeed."

Ralph Waldo Emerson was a great poet, wonderful philosopher and noted historian. Unfortunately, he knew very little about getting a calf into the barn. One day he was actively engrossed in this endeavor.

His son, Edward, circled an arm around the neck of the calf and Emerson pushed from behind. The more they pushed and pulled, the more obstinate the heifer became. The calf locked his knees, dug his feet into the ground and became immovable.

Frustrated, exhausted, and full of bovine smell, the great intellectual was on the verge of losing control.

An Irish peasant girl had been observing the ordeal from a distance and approached Mr. Emerson, "Could I be of assistance," she offered. I can imagine Mr. Emerson was thinking, "If you think you can do anything, go ahead." Smiling softly, she circled around the calf and thrust a finger in the calf's mouth. The calf instinctively followed the girl into the barn.

Edward grinned. Emerson was stunned. After pondering what he had observed, Emerson recorded the incident in his journal followed by this declaration: "I like people who can do things!"

People are like that calf. You can push them, prod them, pull them, yell at them, kick them but they aren't going to move.

Why?

It's because people do things for their reasons, not your reasons. People do things because they want to not because you think it would be a good idea.

Face it. It is easier to get people to do what they want to do than what you want them to do. If you want somebody to do something, you must give them a reason...one of their reasons.

"A wise administrator," suggested Lao Tsu, "does not lead people to set their hearts upon what they cannot have, but satisfies their inner needs."

Questions to Ponder:
1. What do your people need to feel good about their ability to contribute to the team?
2. What do your people need to feel good about their jobs?

More Than a Ribbon

Genuinely Recognize People To The Maximum And Then Double It

Simon Sinek offered this simple leadership strategy; "A boss wants to pay for results, an employee wants recognition for effort. If a boss recognizes effort, they will get even better results."

Let's examine this a bit further...

Jack Roy aspired to be a professional comedian. Unfortunately, his audiences didn't send a supportive message, rarely laughing at his performances.

Disappointed, he resumed his earlier career as a salesperson.

At age 40, Jack decided to give the comedic gig one more try. This time, his self-deprecating humor caused audiences to embrace his lack of success, recognize his need to be appreciated and playfully acknowledge his quest to overcome repeated failure.

His comic refrain, "I don't get no respect," became his mantra, and Jack Roy - or Rodney Dangerfield, as he is better known - became a hit and connected with audiences across the nation.

Feeling unappreciated is nothing new!

Rodney Dangerfield struck a chord with countless people who previously were fearful of expressing the ungratefulness they felt at work. Feeling unappreciated and taken for granted is a universal negative emotion experienced in countless work environments.

In Globeforce's employee "Mood Tracker" survey, 94% of employees said they like getting recognized for accomplishments at work. Similarly, 82 percent said that getting recognized for efforts at work motivates them in their jobs.

For years the ribbon industry has thrived on people's need for recognition. There are ribbons to recognize every conceivable achievement (even 12th Place), contribution or special designation.

Unfortunately, Ribbon Recognition is SOOOO temporary!

What Rodney Dangerfield ultimately experienced was intrinsic reward. The acceptance, appreciation and applause of the audience.

Think about it, leaders!

Accept people for who they are. Their blemishes. Potential. Quirks. Unconventional approaches. In fact, celebrate the fact your team isn't comprised of clones but individuals who all make a unique contribution to your success.

Appreciation comes in all shapes and sizes. Figure out what appeals to your individual team members. One size certainly does not fit all.

Appreciation naturally appreciates people's value to the team.

Applaud anything you want repeated. Say "thank you," "I'm grateful for your dedication," "That was Fabulous," or "I am so thankful for all you do" every time you have an opportunity.

Accentuate the Positive. Countless leaders are experts at identifying what is wrong with their team members but totally inept at seeing the good.

Genuinely appreciate people to the maximum...and then double it.

Alan Loy McGinnis reminds us that, "When someone comes along who genuinely thanks us, we will follow that person a very long way."

Questions to Ponder:
1. Is appreciation a way of life in our culture? If not, what can we do? If so, how can we improve?
2. How can we accentuate three positives for every one negative?

Creating a New Normal

Travel The Path Of Innovation And Avoid The Ruts Of Normalcy

Scott Belsky is right. "The inspiration to generate ideas comes easy, but the inspiration to take action is more rare."

Can you imagine growing up in the Disney home? I have no clue what Walt's childhood was like, but his brother gives us a glimpse into their world and Walt's creative determination.

In the fifth grade, Walt's teacher assigned the class to color a flower garden. The students diligently began their work as the teacher wandered the rows examining each student's work. Walt's flower garden differed from the other students. He drew faces on his flowers.

"Walt, that's not how we color flowers. Flowers don't have faces on them."

Young Walt confidently replied, "Mine Do!" and continued his 'incorrect' masterpiece.

Well, Walt's flowers continued to have faces on them and still do; at Disney World and Disneyland.

Fortunately, Walt Disney didn't let the discouragement of a few people or what was considered to be a typical flower to hamper his creative aptitude.

Don't let what's considered normal stop you from creating a new normal or even better, abnormal.

There are enormous benefits realized by combining a minute amount of innovation with a spoonful of pragmatic passion. It's okay to put faces on your flowers.

Despite the undeniably positive benefits of innovation within organizations, it seems that multiple detours, roadblocks and warning signs frequently surface to squelch creativity. People need permission to create. Sad!

According to a UCLA study, at age five, we engage in creative tasks 98 times a day, laugh 113 times and ask questions 65 times. (No wonder we have so much fun as kids). By the age of 44, however, the number shrinks to 2 creative tasks a day, 11 laughs, and 6 questions. (No wonder kids don't want to grow up).

In addition, the UCLA study found a 91 percent negative response rate among adults exposed to new ideas. Seriously!?

Creativity and innovation flourish in an environment that encourages them to sprout and blossom, but all it takes is a frown or a negative word to shut them down completely.

My role (your role) as a leader is to nourish, encourage and nurture the creative spirit.

Never fear traveling the path of innovation but avoid the ruts of normalcy at all costs. Follow the path defined by Mary Lou Cook: "Creativity is inventing, experimenting, growing, taking risks, breaking rules, making mistakes, and having fun."

Questions to Ponder:
1. What was your last idea? Did you pursue it? Why or why not?
2. What is an unthinkable thing to do right in your organization but if you did it, it would have a dramatic impact on the quality of what you do?

What's "Just Right?"

Live On The Cutting Edge Of Fresh And Exciting Prospects

As a young boy, I was fascinated by fairy tales. One of my favorites was Goldilocks and the Three Bears. You remember the story line. The three bears lived in a small suburb on the city's outskirts. On one bright sunny morning, the bear family journeyed into the city to do a little shopping at the mall. (O.K., I admit it...I've changed the story slightly to fit the current times).

While away, a young girl named Goldilocks rode up to the bear's suburban home on her ten-speed bike. She peeked through each paned glass window and rang the chiming doorbell. Unable to arouse anyone's attention, Goldilocks easily entered through the back door and into the family's kitchen.

Noticing three bowls neatly set at the country style table, Goldilocks tasted the contents of the first bowl. It was far too hot! The cereal in the second bowl was too cold! However, the third bowl's cereal was JUST RIGHT. Goldilocks devoured the contents.

Making her way to the living room, Goldilocks noticed three beautifully stuffed chairs. Testing the largest overstuffed chair, Goldilocks didn't feel comfortable. The medium sized wing-backed chair was not much better. However, the third smaller chair was JUST RIGHT... until it collapsed. Frightened by the sound of snapping pine, Goldilocks quickly ran up the stairs.

The upstairs was one large bedroom suite, containing three neatly made beds in varying sizes. Goldilocks stretched her small frame on the largest bed. It was far too hard to suit her liking. The medium sized bed was cushiony soft but sagged in the middle. The third and smallest bed provided adequate support, was the perfect size and the bedspread colors matched Goldilocks' sundress. This bed was JUST RIGHT, and Goldilocks fell fast asleep.

Visionary people are willing to experiment to find out what's JUST RIGHT. They are committed to break through the status quo, create a new way of life and live on the cutting edge of fresh and exciting prospects.

WARNING! Goldilocks wasn't perfect. Although determined to find what was JUST RIGHT, she became so comfortable she fell asleep. Leaders, too, must be careful of the tendency to become trapped in their contentment.

There are no shortages of opportunities for leaders who want to make a difference; for those compelled to make things 'just right'. The challenges facing business, education, communities, and churches cry out for leaders with the determination and vision to alter the status quo.

Leaders passionate about making a difference are people devoted to helping their organization be better tomorrow than they are today. They capitalize on the opportunity to move from mediocrity into greatness. These are the leaders with a vision for the future with no intent of becoming 'comfortable.'

"As a visionary leader," observed Sheila Murray Bethel "you'll find beauty where others do not. You'll seek opportunity where others find only problems, and you'll see answers where others haven't yet recognized the questions."

Visionary leaders create a culture that celebrates newness…the search for what's "just right."

They possess an unwavering desire to address today's challenges and create within their organization a readiness to respond. Visionary lives are stimulated by a continual desire to be better today than they were yesterday, and they encourage people to follow their example. As a result, these leaders achieve extraordinary results and make it possible for their people to do the same.

"Before we can build great companies," suggests Simon Sinek, "we have to imagine them. Great work always starts with a great vision of the future."

Questions to Ponder:
1. Where can you experiment to find out what's 'just right?'
2. Are there areas where contentment is more prevalent than creativity?

Alone You Are Weak

Single Mindedness Generates Compounded Results.

_____

"I often think about Vance Havner's observation that, "Snowflakes are frail, but if enough of them stick together, they can stop traffic." Living in the Midwest, this observation about snowflakes contains realistic significance.

The story is told of an aging Greek father who was sure he had a short time to live. It was important to him that his sons carry on their lives within the teachings he had tried to instill. The Greek father called his sons together and gave each of them a stick saying: "Break it." From the youngest to the oldest, each son easily broke their stick in half.

The father then took the fourteen pieces, gave the bundle to his youngest son and said, "Break it." He could not. Then the second son was asked to do the same. He could not break the bundle of fourteen sticks. Nor could any of the rest of the sons.

Reflecting on his son's experience, the wise father advised, "Always remember, "alone you are weak, together you are strong."

Author and teamwork expert Patrick Lencioni said: "If you could get all the people in an organization rowing in the same direction, you could dominate any industry in any market, against any competition, at any time."

Imagine the incredible force that is created if everyone on your team understands the "why" of what they do. Single mindedness generates compounded energy far beyond what the normal team will experience.

Teams committed to working together toward a common purpose and tap the individual talents of their teammates create a strong, unbreakable, unstoppable bond. The best part is, the combined strength of any team brings increased strength to each individual effort.

You've heard sportscasters refer to outstanding players as being in the "zone." When a team performs flawlessly, announcers may refer to them as being in a "league of their own." Talented players, all tapping their strengths and investing their energies in a common purpose combine to produce impressive results.

This is good stuff and worth any leader's time to determine how they can get their team united with each member headed in the same direction and willing to invest everything they have for the benefit of the team.

That's powerful!

Basketball Hall of Fame coach Phil Jackson is so right:

"The strength of the team is each individual member. The strength of the member is the team."

Questions to Ponder:
1. What's our common purpose? Are we all headed in the same direction?
2. What percent of our team know, understand and are passionate about our purpose?
3. Are people working in their "zone?"

No Correspondence School for Swimmers
You Can't Lead People To Places You Haven't Been

Entrepreneur Richard Branson acknowledged, "My biggest motivation? Just to keep challenging myself. I see life almost like one long university education that I never had–everyday I'm learning something new." Why is Branson's attitude about continual learning and growth so important for any leader? Because, you can't lead people to places you haven't been. People can only grow as far as you have grown.

Growing leaders grow people.
Stagnate leaders stagnate people.
Growing companies require growing leaders.

If you're not growing, your team isn't growing. If you're stalled, your team is stalled. If you plateau, so do they.

As the leader goes, so does the team.

Are you continually growing and refining your skills? Are you challenging yourself with new avenues of experience or ways of thinking? If not, your team hears the same thing regurgitated over and over.

If there is nothing new, innovative, challenging or paradigm shifting going on in your head, there is nothing freshly inspiring coming out of your mouth.

There should be a cardinal rule for leaders that reads:

"If you're as good as you're going to be, you can't be the leader."

Team members deserve much more.

If you want to increase the potential of your team, you need to be actively pursuing your potential. You teach what you know, but you reproduce what you are. You can't give people what you don't have.

To grow, you must be intentional. Leaders who depend on haphazard, accidental learning rarely fine tune their skills enough to grow other people. It takes discipline, focus and energy to raise your abilities and thinking to a new level.

Howard Hendricks has correctly discovered; "There is no such thing as a correspondence course for swimming." Leaders are required to jump into unknown waters, so they can help others experience the thrill of learning and growing.

Nurture a growth mentality which requires an insatiable appetite for learning, experimenting, discovering, listening and never being satisfied with having arrived.

A growth mentality continually perpetuates a fresh perspective, innovative ideas and results exceeding the limits of your goals.

_____

Questions to Ponder:
1. What's the last book you read that inspired you to new levels of performance? What is the one message that resonated with you? What did you do with that inspiration?
2. Who challenges you to new levels of performance? Buy them lunch.
3. How has your growth mentality impacted others

Good People Deserve...

Time and Energy Invested on the Front End Significantly Impacts Rear End Results.

Sir Arthur Conan Doyle, creator of the world-famous detective Sherlock Holmes, reportedly told of a time he was waiting at a taxi stand outside the railway station in Paris. When a taxi pulled up, he placed his suitcase in the car and took a seat next to it.

"Where can I take you, Mr. Doyle?" asked the taxi driver.

Doyle was flabbergasted. He asked the driver if he knew him by sight.

"No sir, I have never seen you before," the driver responded.

The puzzled Doyle asked how he knew he was Conan Doyle.

"This morning's paper had a story about you being on vacation in Marseilles. This is the taxi stand where people who return from

Marseilles always come. Your skin color tells me you have been on vacation. The ink-spot on your right index finger suggests to me that you are a writer. Your clothing is very English, not French. Adding up all those pieces of information, I deduced that you are Sir Arthur Conan Doyle."

Doyle remarked, "This is truly amazing! You are a real-life counter-part to my fictional creation, Sherlock Holmes."

"There was one other clue," the driver said.

"What was that?

"Your name is on the front of your suitcase."

If only the clues to hiring good people...the right people, were that obvious.

Donald Keough, Retired President of Coca-Cola warned us to, "Watch out for bright lights that surround themselves with dim bulbs."

Settling for only the best instead of the almost good enough stacks the deck in your favor every time. If you want people who will work hard, perform at their highest level, display a positive attitude and be a team player, then create a selection process that ensures those results.

"If you lead your team, you are responsible to make sure the revolving door moves in such a way that the players who are joining the team are better than those who are leaving," asserted John C. Maxwell.

Time invested on the front end pays long term dividends. It all begins with establishing a proactive, optimistic, aggressive recruitment and hiring mentality.

Questions to Ponder:
1. What was our best hire in the past '3' months? Why?
2. Where did we settle for less than the best? What have been the results of that hire?
3. What is your hiring credo that ensures only the best fit works for you?

To Be Continued...

To Work With Good People

Never Ever Ever Ever Hire The Best Of The Worst.

Here's some great insight from long-time NBA Coach and Manager Red Auerbach: "How you select people is more important than how you manage them once they're on the job. If you start with the right people, you won't have problems later on. If you hire the wrong people...you're in serious trouble."

The right people are the key to taking any team performance to the next level. Here are some of my random thoughts on making that happen:

Never hire the "best of the worst." Five people come in to apply for a job. None of them are stars but hey, we need to fill a position. So, we hire "the best of the worst." Dave Anderson believes, "Hiring is a lot like dating: As desperation sets in, standards fall!" Bad mistake!

The worst time to hire someone is when you need them. Position yourself in a continual hunt for top talent. Snatch them when you can.

Your greatest recruitment tool is to become the 'preferred employer' in your community. If your current team isn't excited about working with you, there are very few people in the community who will be inspired to join the ranks.

Law of Attraction: You attract what you are, not what you want. Are you a place people are willing to promote without question, hesitation or doubt? If not, you're not too attractive.

Hire People You Would Like Your Kids to Work With.

Recruit – Re Recruit – Re Re Recruit: The key to hiring and retention. If you don't understand it, you don't have it.

The person you interview is never the person you hire.

Generally speaking; want-ads attract the frustrated, terminated, transferred and searching. See Law of Attraction.

Better Players Make Better Players Better.

Every Interview is a "Public Relations Moment."

If you hire right on the front end, carefully selecting the best of the best instead of the best of the worst, you won't waste valuable time and energy desperately trying to change someone from who they are to who you want them to be. That's an exercise in futility!

Warren Buffet reminds us, "If you are going to hire someone that doesn't have character, you had better hope they are dumb & lazy or they will do a lot of stupid things."

If you want to hire the best of the best, the ones with positive attitudes, joyful spirits, enormous talent and compassion, then you must never forget that they can get a job anytime, anywhere. You'll have to have something special for them to come to you.

_____

Questions to Ponder:
1. Read through the suggestions once or twice or more. Have a conversation with at least three other people about these little thought provokers. Use a few of them as springboards for better ideas. Then, identify 1-3 changes you will make to create a culture of hiring excellence.
2. Again, what is your hiring credo?

Eliciting Greatness

Every Life is Capable of Greatness

Condoleezza Rice, former U.S. Secretary of State, believes there is no higher honor than a life of leadership. In support of that conviction, she delivered this profound message during a Leadership Summit speech: "Every life is capable of greatness. Our responsibility as leaders is to create opportunities."

Leaders have the weighty privilege of helping people see their potential and believe in the possibilities of their future.

As John Buchan suggested, "The task of leadership is not to put greatness into people, but to elicit, for the greatness is there already."

Mr. Holland's Opus.

What a delightful movie!

It is the story of Glenn Holland, a young aspiring musician who passionately wants to become a big-time composer.

Money gets tight. He needs consistent income to support a family. Mr. Holland reluctantly pursued a position as a teacher so he could still write his music part time.

Little did he know, this job would consume his life. Although he intended it to be a temporary situation, Mr. Holland discovers his passion for sharing his love for music with his students and discovers much about himself. Students embraced and were inspired by Mr. Holland's conviction that music could transform their lives.

Everyone in the theater had to grieve with Mr. Holland when he learned his teaching position was eliminated because of cutbacks. By now Holland is middle age and he realizes he has missed the opportunity to take his symphony to New York and become a noted composer.

Mr. Holland concludes he has wasted his life!

Despondent, depressed and on the verge of bitterness, he shuffles down the hallway preparing for his final walk out of the school. Noise in the auditorium caught his attention and when he peeked in. Dozens and dozens of students whose lives he impacted during his years of teaching had gathered to honor him.

Never underestimate the impact your influence, actions and encouragement are having on people - even if they don't tell you. Like Glenn Holland, we might need to look past ourselves and see a greater good.

I'm embracing Tammy Tibet's, Co-Founder & CEO of She's the First, inspiration to, "Never underestimate your ability to make someone else 'a first.' You could be the first person to support them and believe in their dreams...and that will matter throughout the rest of their lives."

Believe in People. Show them what makes them special.

Like people. Assume the best in people.

Maximize abilities. Every person is a treasure chest of talent. Open it.

Individualize expectations. Get a mental picture of unbelievable expectations for each of your people. Then, draw it out for them.

Nurture success. Give people the freedom to use their energy and talent reserves to perform.

Questions to Ponder:
1. How are you underestimating your impact on people?
2. Believe. Like. Maximize. Individualize. Nurture. Where are you strong? What needs attention?
3. If everyone believed in people like you do, would more people be discovering their greatness?
4. Who is a primary candidate for you to nurture their success?

Hero or Horrible Boss?

Hero Bosses Stimulate And Extract The Best In People

The film Horrible Bosses features three dreadful managers who make their employee's lives miserable. The targeted victims can't quit. They need the money. In their desperation, they devise elaborate, absurd plans to eliminate their tyrannical bosses. The three friends bond together, and the despicable bosses ultimately cause their own destruction.

In life, the plot is rarely as dramatic or entertaining...or 'happy ever after.'

The movie is an exaggerated (I hope) display of calloused, uncaring, self-indulging, and controlling scenarios that exemplify the potential destruction caused by horrible bosses.

Here's how to be a hero rather than a horrible boss:

Develop People One At A Time.

John Maxwell reminds us, "Never forget that leadership is the art of helping people change from who they thought to be to who they ought to be."

People-focused leaders invest their time, energy, and resources into developing people into all they can become. Nurture the skills, knowledge, and talents of your people and impressive results will follow. Figure out what you can do through training, encouragement, coaching, and mentoring to help your people achieve what they can achieve.

Maximize Individual Strengths.

Author Stephen Covey suggested, "The job of a leader is to build a complementary team; where every strength is made effective and each weakness is made irrelevant."

Great bosses understand people's greatest potential is achieved by maximizing what they're already good at doing. Find out what comes naturally to your team members and discover opportunities for them to excel. Strategically discovering avenues for people to apply what they do best is a fast track for developing high performers.

Nurture a People-Focused Culture.

Impressive leaders create a great people-focused culture that produces remarkable people results. Gary Kelly, Chairman, President and CEO of Southwest Airlines said in the company's September 2011 issue of Spirit that "The biggest difference between Southwest and the rest was the attention to Culture. Your business plan is what you are, but Culture is who you are."

A people-focused culture evolves out of a leader's inherent respect for people and a desire for people to truly be the priority.

Believe in People.

Every supervisor has someone who is yearning to find a leader who believes in them more than they believe in themselves. Find that person. Be that leader.

Before giving up on a challenged team member, pour your full effort into them. Inject some confidence. Reassure them that you believe they can excel and you're there to help them get to where they want to go.

Norman Schwarzkopf suggested: "People go to work to succeed not to fail. It's the leader's duty and responsibility to lead people to success."

Sometimes you're successful. Sometimes not. Give it your best shot. Sometimes, the victory is just knowing you tried.

When you're successful . . . you'll be a hero and will have gained a team member prepared to perform at new heights.

Serve. Serve. Serve.

The higher you rise, the greater your opportunity to serve and the greater your obligation to find ways to encourage, elevate and energize those around you.

Assume a servant role in all matters, treating others as the most important person in your life.

In their book The Leadership Challenge, James Kouzes and Barry Posner write, "Any leadership practice that increases another's sense of self-confidence, self-determination, and personal effectiveness makes that person more powerful and greatly enhances the possibility of success."

The strategies to become a hero rather than a horrible boss are rather simplistic – but profound!

One day a little boy approached Walt Disney and asked, "Do you draw Mickey Mouse?"

Walt humbly admitted, "I don't draw anymore."

The little boy continued, "Then you think up all the jokes and ideas?"

"No," Disney responded, "I don't do that."

Quizzically the boy looked at Disney and said, "Mr. Disney, just what do you do?

"Well," Disney graciously responded, "sometimes I think of myself as a little bee, I go from one area of the studio to another and gather pollen and sort of stimulate everybody. I guess that's the job I do."

Hero bosses nurture everyone around them by stimulating and extracting the best that is available.

Questions to Ponder:
1. Does your culture warrant you being considered a leadership hero?
2. What areas could be improved?

What's Your Leadership Approach?
Be The Leader You Would Want Your Children To Work For

Max DuPree's leadership writings are simple, profound, practical and enlightening. Here's an example: "Leadership, as you know, is not a position but a job. It's hard and exciting and good work. It's also a serious meddling in other people's lives. One examines leadership beginning not with techniques but rather with premises, not with tools but with beliefs, and not with systems but with understandings."

...a serious meddling in people's lives.

When speaking of General John Fremont, prior to firing him, Abraham Lincoln made the following observation, "His cardinal mistake is that he isolates himself and allows nobody to see him and by which, he does not know what is going on in the very matters that he's dealing with."

Forbes writer George Bradt observed that, "One of the most

fundamental lessons of leadership is that if you're a leader, it's not about you. It's about the people following you. The best leaders devote almost all their energy to inspiring and enabling others. Taking care of them is a big part of this."

Leadership is not about you as much as the people you are responsible for.

I've surmised there are several "ssive" approaches to leadership. Some good. Some not so good. All express our prominent "beliefs" and "premises."

Progressive. Progressive leaders are incessantly pursuing 'what could be,' including challenging and mastering their own leadership competency. Sometimes you need to do something outside YOUR comfort zone to get people to come along side you.

Create a vision for the future. Articulate it so people know where you're going. Become a creator of liberating visions, a reinforcer of hope, and an example of action. Life begins where your comfort zone ends.

Expressive. Leaders who inspire greatness possess a generous serving of irrational exuberance that stimulates others to challenge their personal and professional thinking and performance boundaries…to consider unthinkable possibilities.

Expressive leaders freely allow others to see and experience their heartfelt emotions about things that really matter. In fact, their passion gives permission to everyone around them to express their passion.

Impressive. A leader's role is to raise people's aspirations for what they can become and to release their energies so they will try to get there. That's impressive!

Ralph Lauren believes, "A leader has the vision and conviction that a dream can be achieved. He inspires the power and energy to get it done."

When you give people what they need, instead of what they presently want, to achieve their ambitions, hopes and dreams, you'll naturally be an impressive leader.

Impressive leaders are trench dwellers. They dig in with their teammates to ensure the best possible outcomes.

Suppressive. Tom Peters reminds us, "It's horrifying how easy it is to de-motivate someone—to dent/diminish/destroy their fragile psychological ownership of a task!"

In their book The Manager's Communication Handbook, the authors share these disturbing findings: First, only 14% of employees said they had a positive role model at work. Also, 86% couldn't identify even one person at work they wanted to emulate. How sad! Especially considering these attitudes are a direct hit on leaders.

Identify and eliminate any action or attitude that causes people to be skittish, discouraged or hope depleted.

Digressive. "Explosive, erratic behavior by leadership does not inspire; on the contrary, not knowing what to expect is one of the greatest causes of organizational paralysis," believes Dave Ramsey. "When people can't predict how you will react, they freeze and do nothing."

Digression is an unavoidable outcome. Get your emotional act together.

Possessive. Yikes! Controlling leaders are really a nuisance. Every time progress is about to happen, they show up to stymie the process. Their controlling nature makes progress possible only when the process follows their way of doing things. These 'snoopervisors' believe their possessive spirit encourages people to put their best foot forward. Not so much.

Obsessive. Truett Cathy (Chick-Fil-A Founder) indicated, "the number one reason leaders are unsuccessful is their inability to lead themselves." Effective leaders are obsessed with continual personal and professional development. They understand, everyone gets better when the leader gets better.

Obsessive leaders are passionate about making every minute count in their life by growing, learning and leading.

Oppressive. Domineering. Harsh. Unfair. How are you leading? Are you challenging your people? Are you gently pushing them outside their comfort zone? Are you preparing them for a great future – or not a future at all? Oppressive leaders are preoccupied with themselves. Their power. Their authority.

Personally, I lean toward two pieces of advice when determining the "ssive" type leader I need to be.

First, be the type of leader you would love your children to work for.

Second, be the leader you wish you had.

Questions to Ponder:
1. Are you the type of leader you would like your children to work for?
2. What's it like to be led by you?
3. What "ssive" style do you most associate with? Which would you like to emulate more?

Pulling Together

Team Achievements Always Outshine Individual Accomplishments.

Outstanding organizational achievements are the result of the combined collaborative efforts of everyone on the team. Creating and maintaining high-producing, cooperative teams is an exciting challenge. Just keep in mind this valuable motivator; that alone you are good, but together, you can be the best in the world.

Reid Hoffman, the cofounder and chairman of LinkedIn, summed it: "No matter how brilliant your mind or strategy, if you're playing a solo game, you'll always lose out to a team."

When I was growing up in a small town in central South Dakota, Summer vacation basically involved two activities—baseball and swimming. However, late in the Summer a special event came to town. Everybody and their cat attended the County Fair.

At one county fair the main attraction was a horse-pulling contest. Contestants brought in the strongest horses in the county to compete. The race involved hitching one horse at a time to a weighted down sled. As the horse began to pull, additional weight was added until the horse was unable to take another step. The horse that pulled the most weight won.

At this horse pulling contest the winning horse pulled 9111 pounds. The second-place horse pulled 9087 pounds. This was the closest contest the judges had witnessed in years. The difference between first and second place was only 24 pounds, which is peanuts when you think about the 9000 pounds these horses were pulling.

The judges wondered what would happen if they took the first and second place horses, gave them some oats and water and allowed them time to rest. Then, hitch them both to the same sled. How much weight would they be able to pull together?

Arrangements were made to offer the bonus event. The crowd (consisting of predominantly frugal Dutch people) were excited about getting two events for the price of one.

The two horses were brought back onto the track and hitched to the same sled. They pulled with brute force. Eight legs churned furiously throwing clods of dirt high into the air. Spectators sat in awe as weight and more weight and more weight was added to the sled until the horses were unable to take another step.

The judges immediately untied the horses and began the task of determining how much the two horses together could pull. Everyone was startled and cheered in unison as the final tally was announced. Together, the two horses had pulled 31,247 pounds. Not only had this twosome put on quite a show, they were able to pull three and one-half times the weight they pulled individually.

I believe dynamic teams can achieve three and one-half times what an individual team member can achieve. They can be three and a half times more effective, produce three and a half times the quality and productivity team members can realize on their own.

What would have happened if one horse said, "Look, I've been in seven contests this summer and second place is the best I've attained. Why in the world should I go back out and pull alongside a horse who wins every race they enter?" Or the first-place horse decides it has done just fine by himself. Why go out and pull with a horse whose record can't light a candle to his? Or what if one horse decided to run one way while the other went the opposite direction? What might have happened if one horse gave 100% effort while the second horse decided to slough? The results would have been disastrous.

These horses, in their own horse language, decided to give their best for the success of the team. The true measure of cooperation is not exceptional individual achievements but team members combining their efforts to better the organization. Cooperation is the natural outcome of the organization's culture and operating personality. Just like the horse-pulling contest, the success of your team is dependent on the 100% cooperative effort of each individual team member.

As Steve Jobs learned, "Great things in business are never done by one person. They're done by a team of people." Remember: Alone you are good, but together, you can be the best in the world.

_____

Questions to Ponder:
1. Is your team accomplishing 3 1/2 times what everyone could on their own?
2. What factors tend to inhibit collaboration and productivity?

Engaged? Disengaged?

You Can't Force Engagement. Create A Culture That Nourishes It.

Here's a reality check from leadership expert Frances Hesselbein "Dispirited, unmotivated, unappreciated workers cannot compete in a highly competitive world."

On the flip side, encouraged, enabled, empowered, enthused, energized and engaged people will be winners in this highly competitive world.

Gallup surveys millions of people, in thousands of companies, to determine the state of engagement of today's American workforce. Results from their 2012 survey leave something to be desired.

52% of American workers are **Not Engaged**. They're sleepwalking through their workday–putting in time, but not energy or passion, into their work.

13% are **Actively Disengaged.** They aren't just unhappy at work; they're busy acting out their unhappiness. Every day, these workers undermine what their engaged coworkers accomplish.

35% are **Engaged.** Work with passion and feel a profound connection to their company. They drive innovation and move the organization forward. These team members go the extra mile because of their strong emotional connection to the organization. Engagement goes beyond a merely satisfactory experience at work to one of 100% psychological commitment.

Great data! Wonderful information! Why is it important to leaders?

Gallup has consistently found that leaders play a significant role in driving employee engagement. They also discovered that leaders who focus on employee's strengths can practically eliminate active disengagement. In my humble opinion, that is exciting stuff!

There are consistent traits and behaviors displayed by great leaders who engage people.

1. Build strong, trusting relationships which engender an open and honest environment.

An engaging environment owes its success to many factors, but collaborative relationships are the epitome of this culture. Any leader passionate about influencing people into the future understands the critical nature of building a relationship with their team in the now. Without relationships, what's the purpose of leadership?

2. Display genuine care and concern for people.

Care just as much about people as individuals as you do about their performance. The new workforce proposition: Take better care of us and we'll take better care of business. Be more concerned about who people are rather than what they do.

3. Value and Invest in Talent.

Engaging leaders position people in areas/tasks that will use their greatest strengths. Gallup found that just knowing their strengths makes team members 7.8% more productive. However, when leaders focus on strengths every day, their team members are 12.5% more productive.

Remember what it was like when you got 'engaged' to be married? That's what 'engage'ment is all about - excitement, anticipation, commitment, ownership...

You can't force it, but you can create a culture that nourishes it.

Let's make it happen!

Questions to Ponder:

1. What 2 things can you do today to impact the engagement of your team members?

Never Stop Believing

Make Your Culture A Place Where People Are Invited To Excel.

When my daughter Katy was in the sixth grade, she asked me to coach a group of her friends who wanted to play basketball. We assembled a team of ten girls and began practicing the fundamentals of basketball. Unfortunately, the girls were not natural athletes, but they had a lot of heart. For some unknown reason, they named themselves the Bullets.

By the time our first tournament rolled around, I was a bit suspect of what the outcome might be. Our first game was against a very mature, polished, athletic sixth grade team who cleaned our clock.
Final score: 56 – 4.

In the second game, we drew a fifth-grade team from the same community as our last opponent who were certainly more experienced than we were. It was a depressing, long, deflating game.
Final score: 54 – 6.

Our girls were devastated! In unison, they all declared their desire to give up basketball. In between tears I attempted to put a band aid on the hurt pride but my attempt at consoling them was futile. Once the emotions subsided, I had an opportunity to inject some optimism.

"Listen girls, it's just your first tournament and I know you can get better. Meet me at the gym Monday evening at 6:00 and we're going to start becoming a basketball team," I said.

On Monday evening, we all sat on the gym floor and discussed our strategy. "I believe in you girls. I see you in the future and you look much better than you did last Saturday. I know we can become a good basketball team. Here are the three things that will guide our team from now on.

First, whether you are on the court or on the bench, you are all going to positively encourage one another. If you decide to become critical of a teammate, you will be invited to sit on the bench next to me. You don't want that. We will win together and lose together and always encourage each other.

Secondly, we are going to have fun. That's why we started the team. When it is no longer fun, I don't want to be the coach.

The third important element is going to help us have fun and play basketball the right way. We are going to learn basketball fundamentals.

Learning basketball fundamentals, supporting each other and having fun guided us through every practice, near win games, getting trounced and our periodic wins.

I wish I could tell you these girls became super stars. They didn't. But they did learn basketball fundamentals, how to play as a team and win or lose to have fun together. I was so proud of how each girl left their heart on floor every game they played. As a bonus, in their third year together they won 12 games and lost 6. They even took second place in a tournament. They were elated. Ecstatic!

I am proud of the fact that I made our practices, games, and relationships a place where the girls were invited to excel. They learned to believe in themselves. We just removed some of the previous roadblocks to success and gave them the tools that made success possible. I never stopped believing in them.

Jumpstarting people performance means expanding a person's view of themselves, raising their performance to an elevated standard, and helping them grow beyond their self-conceived limitations.

Simply stated, the greatest way for people to become inspired to raise their level of performance is to believe in themselves. When leaders choose the right people, provide exceptional orientation and training, and inspire them to stretch toward their potential, the stage is set for quite a performance. Find out where your people can excel and push them to their highest level.

The leader's task is to create a culture conducive to self-motivation and superior performance. Buy into this philosophy and your leadership effectiveness and the performance of your team will improve dramatically.

Questions to Ponder:
1. How can you expand a team member's view of themselves?
2. What roadblocks to success can you remove for people?

Future Fascination

A Fascination With Tradition Can Result In Extinction

Throngs of people are in love with tradition and go to great extremes to hang on to 'what is.' They simply don't want to admit that times are changing and refuse to buy into the thought that they will need to make any adjustments.

I reflect on companies like Sears, Blockbuster, Radio Shack, BlackBerry, Kodak (there's a theme here) who were convinced their business model was impenetrable.

Hmmmm.

At one time, these companies endeared the respect of countless customers and Wall Street admirers. Unfortunately, blinded by their own success and blindsided by other company's innovations, they faltered and failed. Tradition, not innovation drove them to unavoidable extinction.

Seth Godin reminds us that, "Transformational leaders don't start by denying the world around them. Instead, they describe a future they'd like to create instead."

My mind gravitates toward Intel, Apple, Google, Facebook, Amazon who all seem to understand their supremacy is only as secure as the innovative future they are envisioning and constructing. Leaders in these companies are not allowing their teams to sit on their hands and think they can forever enjoy the fruits of yesterday's efforts.

Consider Marcus Buckingham's suggestion; "Leaders are fascinated by future. You are a leader if and only if, you are restless for change, impatient for progress and deeply dissatisfied with status quo. Because in your head, you can see a better future. The friction between 'what is' and 'what could be' burns you, stirs you up, propels you. This is leadership."

If you retired today, would you be remembered as a leader who embraced the future and continually refined your image of what the future would look like? Or, remembered as the one who fell in love with the status quo and warmly allowed others to do the same?

Tennis great Roger Federer embraced a healthy mentality about success. "I always questioned myself in the best of times," he said, "even when I was world number one for many, many weeks and months in a row. At certain times during the year I said, 'What can I improve? What do I need to change? Because if you don't do anything or you just do the same thing over and over again, you stay the same and staying the same means going backward."

Great message: don't be consumed or too impressed with past success. Keep asking what needs to get better so we don't stagnate and cause our own demise.

Reshaping the present and shaping the future are imperative for continued success and even survival.

Bill Gates believes, "Success today requires the agility and drive to constantly rethink, reinvigorate, react and reinvent."

Questions to Ponder:
1. When is the last time I changed anything in my daily routine?
2. How is my vision of the future different than the reality of the present? What am I doing to bridge the gap?

Beyond a Poster

Mission Provides The Why Behind The What.

_____

A little boy approached his mommy with this question: "Mommy, is it true that we come from dust and some day we return to dust?"

"Yes, that's what I believe," his mother responded.

"Then," said the little boy, "there is someone under my bed, but I don't know if he is coming or going."

Countless teams experience the same confusion - unsure if they are coming or going. While questioning the direction of their efforts, they wander aimlessly searching for a reason for what they do.

Did you know one of the main reasons people under perform is that they don't know 'why' they are doing what they are doing? I can't imagine not understanding the 'why' behind my daily activity and how I am contributing in some small way to the overall success of the company.

A solid mission, a sense of purpose provides the unquestionable direction that teams need to know if they are 'coming or going.'

No organization, small or large, can succeed over the long haul without energized team members who believe in, understand and are passionate about living the mission.

Leader - your job is to become comfortable with seeing actions, performance and events in your organization through the lens of the mission, vision and values. Without sounding too philosophical, you need to develop a meaningful personal relationship with the mission, so it is the compelling force for everything you do.

How can you make the mission jump off the page of the poster into real life?

Consider Winston Churchill. During his first speech as prime minister in the House of Commons, he declared his powerful obsession: "You ask; what is our Aim?" I can answer that in one word; 'Victory'. Victory at all costs, victory in spite of terror, victory however long and hard the road may be: for without victory there is no survival."

Churchill left little doubt what the purpose was, and everyone knew 'why' they were doing what they were called to do. Victory!

You ask, what is our purpose? Why do we do what we do? What does my job have to do with purpose anyway?

Leader—what is your passionate response?

This may all sound a bit theoretical and to some degree, it is. Yet, a well-embraced mission serves leaders by providing direction, meaning, and a sense of coherence to everything they do.

Mission is a power-producing, directional tool that gives people the 'why' behind the 'what.'

Questions to Ponder:

1. How will you make the mission the powerful tool it is intended to be?

Give It To Me Straight

If the Communicator is Unable to Communicate Clearly, the Hearer will be Unable to Comprehend Clearly.

I'm intrigued and entertained by the DirecTV commercials that start with "When you have cable..." and end with something ridiculous.

The writers of these commercials apparently never read Winston Churchill's admonition: "If you have an important point to make, don't try to be subtle or clever. Use a pile driver."

Remember this one?

When you have cable and can't find something good to watch, you get depressed. When you get depressed, you attend seminars. When you attend seminars, you feel like a winner. When you feel like a winner, you go to Vegas. When you go to Vegas, you lose everything. And when you lose everything, you sell your hair to a wig shop. Don't sell your hair to a wig shop; get rid of cable, and upgrade to DirecTV.

The commercial certainly makes the point that one bad decision can lead to outcomes of greater negative implication.

In the workplace, this form of communication might cause significant "guessing." What do they mean? What's the real message? Are they telling us we should never go to Vegas? Have they cancelled attending seminars for fear we might become winners?

Professor Howard Hendricks tells his seminary students, "If it's a mist in the pulpit, it will be a fog in the pew." Believe me, a slightly confusing message from the lips of a leader will ultimately result in mass confusion among team members.

It's this simple: if the communicator is unable to communicate clearly, the hearer will be unable to comprehend clearly.

Churchill was right, when you have something of significance that needs to be communicated, deliver a clear, concise (no guessing) heartfelt message.

I'm certainly an advocate of diplomacy and communicating important messages with a sense of 'heart.' A Chinese proverb says, "Do not remove a fly from your neighbor's face with a hatchet."

Yikes!

How you say something is probably just as important (if not more important) than the message you are delivering.

Once communicated, there should be perfect clarity about the message thus producing the expected results or actions.

Practice. When you have an important message, find a trusted advisor, an accountability partner and practice delivering the message. Ask for complete honesty!

"Is this how the message should be delivered?" "Am I as clear as clear can be?"

"Will team members walk away with a firm grasp on the issue?"

"What did I miss?"

If it is below you to ask for help effectively communicating messages, then effectively communicating might be above you.

Just saying...

Questions to Ponder:
1. What is the main point of my message?
2. What do I want people to take away from my message?
3. How will I know if I connected with the receivers?
4. What action, emotion do I expect in response?

Unified Leadership Team

Not a Nicety. A Necessity.

If a Leadership Team is not attitudinally and behaviorally unified there is a marginal chance for the organization to be healthy.

Leaders can attempt to manage the other organizational variables but if the leadership team (key leadership people) is dysfunctional, progress is stymied, even digresses.

A unified leadership team is a strategic choice to unite individual experience, expertise, personalities and talents to achieve a common objective, mission, and vision.

Hall of Fame Basketball Coach John Wooden reminded us that "A leader shapes - even sets - the fundamental values and ideals, attitudes, and behavior that flow through and then define an organization." This responsibility is amplified in a leadership team.

Leadership team members should include people who represent key elements of the organization AND bring critical ideas, information and insight to the forefront.

How Do We Get There?

A unified leadership team does not imply everything is honky dory, we hold hands, and stand around the campfire singing kum-ba-ya.

REAL trust & respect on a team means transparency, honesty and vulnerability. Defensiveness, cover your butt, hidden (personal) agendas and excusiology are absent. Each member's ego is in check and the good of the organization is the primary driver.

Secondly, recognize the value and worth of each person we are privileged to encounter, work with and serve. Know each other. Identify **warts,** strengths, dreams, personal stories...see how it all contributes to their value to the team.

Next, seek to understand what is important to others. Why do people act the way they do? What drives them? Where do I struggle with other people's tendencies, behaviors and attitudes? What rationale might they give for their personal profile? What am I overlooking? Where do I need to exercise acceptance and tolerance?

This all begins with the leader. Don't look around waiting for someone else to take the lead. If you're the leader...lead. Admit mistakes, embrace self-deprecating humor, be willing to tell your story, 'expose' yourself. You can't ask others to do what you avoid.

Embrace conflict. Don't embrace conflict for the sake of conflict but as a necessary step in the journey to discovering what's right. See why the first stages of Leadership Team development are so important...without them conflict is purely painful without the potential gains.

Don't pretend everything is okay. Fabricated harmony is destructive to the fabric of teamwork.

I don't have to love conflict - just don't avoid it. Don't pretend collaboration exists when you know there are underlying issues. Recognize the ultimate value it brings to the big picture vision...doing what's right (not determining who's right) for the long term good. In fact, you may need to decide without everyone agreeing—that's called leadership. But you will expect unified implementation.

Conflict can Create Clarity. Clarity nurtures Collaboration even if I don't have Consensus.

Compassionate Accountability - leaders must also take responsibility for confronting all behaviors that negatively impact the culture, relationships or results.

Compassionate Accountability is the ability to communicate the good, the bad and the ugly - with compassion.

Powerful Leadership Teams (or any team for that matter) hold one another accountable to achieve unified, stretching standards. No exceptions!

Reward trust building behavior - listening, encouraging, taking responsibility, appreciating, producing. Commend these behaviors directly and honestly.

Confront, deal with, discipline distrustful behavior like criticizing, gossiping, back-biting, loafing, rule writing, private whispering conversations, sarcasm, and innuendos. Never tolerate or overlook these behaviors.

Key Reality: The more comfortable a leader is embracing compassionate accountability the less frequently they will need to do so.

Ultimately, a leadership team must Prove It! It? Their effectiveness...

Unified, dynamic, effective leadership teams have a clear understanding of expected results and measure their success by the progress they are making.

First, is everyone focused on the same expectations. Do we have unified priorities? Have we even asked?

Do we agree we are 'in it' together and recognize the value of each person's contribution? This is where team silos are eradicated. Anything that jeopardizes our success is the responsibility of everyone. Anything that enhances our success a reason for everyone to celebrate.

Every leader, every department, every team member is solidly focused on the World Class journey and willing to do 'whatever it takes' to help another team, each other and the organization move closer to proving our effectiveness.

Leaders unwilling or unable to adamantly encourage and expect their team to be unified, on the same page, headed in the same direction severely limit their own and the organization's effectiveness.

A Unified Leadership Team is not a Nicety. It is a Necessity!

Questions to Ponder:

1. How would I describe the current effectiveness of our Leadership Team?
2. What will it take to increase our unity?
3. Where could I display more compassionate accountability?

Position People for Success

See The Possibilities In People.

Napoleon Hill keenly observed, "No man ever achieved worthwhile success who did not, at one time or another; find himself with at least one foot hanging well over the brink of failure."

Rare is the person who hasn't felt like they had one foot dangerously close to disaster when someone came along to keep total chaos or calamity from erupting.

Leaders, driven by a passion to help others be successful, will find themselves bailing people out of potential disaster and gently leading them to safety and success.

I begin my week with this simple question:

"What can I do this week to set people up for success? How can I

speak life, hope, and confidence into someone?"

I learned early in my career what a blessing it was to have people around me who sincerely wanted me to be successful. These leaders took a personal interest in my life. They delegated projects they held close to their chest for me to experiment with. Some leaders believed in me when there was no reason to. They always shielded me from potential disaster and pointed me in the direction toward success.

I had a special leader in my early professional life who looked past my deficiencies to my potential. He trusted me with responsibilities beyond my professional competence or comfort level and I felt compelled to prove him right. I had a coach who put me in the game at a critical moment without any hesitation. There was a publisher who took a rookie writer and led him down the road to publishing several books. And today, an owner, who often wonders what I'll try next, gives me the freedom to fail...or succeed.

What's the point? I trusted these people. Those who express faith in us are worthy of our trust. They have communicated an inherent faith in who we are and what we are capable of, and we will certainly do our best not to let them down.

When leaders create a genuinely caring culture, oozing with support, and committed to team member involvement in decisions impacting the direction of their team, people begin to believe they are positioned to do something special. It's not a leadership strategy or program of the month but a lifestyle that permeates everything you do to help people succeed.

I love Ken Blanchard's advice that, "Everyone you meet is a potential winner; some are disguised as losers. Don't be fooled by their appearances."

Exactly!

See the possibilities in people. Be there to care, nurture, mentor, correct and provide opportunities for growth and achievement.

Helping others be successful is a recognized, dynamic, powerful trust builder...not to mention basic leadership dimension.

Believe in people more than they believe in themselves.

Questions to Ponder:

1. Who appears close to 'stepping over the edge?" How can you come along side?
2. What have you done this week to help one of your team members create a win in their life?

A Light Touch

Never do anything for anybody they can do for themselves.

Jockey Willie Shoemaker was once asked the secret to his incredible success. "I keep a light touch on the horse's rein," he said. "It doesn't know I'm there unless he needs me."

That's powerful! It's also remarkably applicable to building high performance people.

"People are empowered," wrote Rick Mauer, "when they are given the authority and responsibility to make decisions affecting their work with a minimum of interference and second guessing."

So often leaders get so wrapped up in people's responsibilities, they end up involved in doing much of the work themselves. In addition to becoming overloaded and overwhelmed, they inadvertently make people dependent on them. People depend on the leader to resolve problems, make decisions, or give the okay to move forward on projects. The leader becomes burned out and their people remain dependent and underdeveloped.

As Max DePree declared, "You've got to abandon your ego to the talents of others." Ouch! 'Light touch' leaders abandon their egos, feel comfortable with not having all the answers, or being the go to person for every decision to be made. Instead, they become the conductor of a finely tuned orchestra of talent.

"A desk is a dangerous place from which to view the world," advised John le Carré. We've all heard about Management by Walking Around (MBWA) but providing guidance goes beyond walking the halls. Take the time to build relationships so you can better determine people's needs. Be willing to hold someone's hand to get them through a challenge—even though sometimes the challenge is getting people to let go.

When I was working with adults with disabilities, one of our cardinal rules was to **never do anything for anybody that they could do for themselves.** By doing 'for' people we take away the privilege and special feeling we get when we accomplish something independently.

I'm old enough for The Andy Griffith Show to have been one of my favorite childhood television programs. Even today, cable television makes it possible to relive this family entertainment. You can still see the ongoing challenge Sheriff Andy experiences attempting to mentor his deputy Barney into a competent police officer.

It seemed every episode involved Andy teaching his assistant the 'whys' and 'how-to's' of life. Then Barney would set out to deal with real situations and mess it up virtually every time. Despite his bumbling personality and mistake prone actions, Andy was always there to counsel, retrain, console and send Barney out to engage the world one more time.

Andy certainly had his fair share of frustration and at times, had to bail Barney out of his precarious situations. (There was a good reason Barney never attained the level of competence that allowed him to go beyond one bullet in his gun.) Even so, Andy refrained from doing 'for' Barney. He displayed a remarkable degree of self-control and remained committed 'to' Barney and his continual development.

Loosen the reins and watch people run...

Questions to Ponder:

1. What things am I doing for people they can do for themselves?
2. In what specific situations could I loosen my grip and maintain a 'light touch?'

Expect the Best

You have to expect it before you can get it!

Expectations communicate, beyond a shadow of a doubt, the level of belief you have in people.

Ralph Waldo Emerson asserted, "Our chief want in life is somebody who will make us do what we can."

When expectations are high, they create a focus that translates into energy. Leaders failing to raise the expectation bar impede people's potential, limit their thinking, restrict their vision, and quietly allow mediocrity to become the standard.

German Writer, Dramatist and Poet Goethe said: "Treat a man as he is, he will remain so." In other words, the way you see people is the way you treat them and the way you treat them is what they become. The parent who sees their two-year old child as being in the "terrible twos" will no doubt communicate that expectation and even excuse their behavior at times due to this stage in their life. Two-year-olds are incredibly smart. They will live up to your every "terrible two" expectation.

Talk about communicating expectations. How about the supervisor who upon hiring a new team member commented: "You've got the job, but we're going to keep the ad running just in case this doesn't work out." There's a confidence builder.

The leaders who constantly complain about their people clearly communicate their expectations. It's amazing how the troublemaker, substandard performer, complainer or proverbial busy body will meet those expectations when the leader believes that's the best they can offer.

Goethe continued: "If I accept you as you are, I will make you worse; however, if I treat you as though you are what you are capable of becoming, I help you become that." He also advised: "Treat a man the way he can be and ought to be, and he will become as he can be and should be."

If you treat people as they are, they will continue as they are. But if you treat people as they can become, they will become what they can become. This is powerful stuff for a leader! Simply stated, it communicates to people that **I see you in the future and you look much better than you look right now.**

One of the best ways to inspire people is to show them who they could be. Jack Nicholson delivers a great line to Helen Hunt in the film As Good as It Gets: "You make me want to be a better man." That's what great leaders do every day…make people want to be better by expecting more from them than they ever thought they could do or be.

You must expect it before you can get it!

Positive expectations communicate hope. Potential. Possibilities. Capabilities. Our degree of commitment and willingness to serve is visible in our expectations of people. See people as they can become then treat them consistent with your new, stretching expectations. You'll be amazed at how people respond.

Peter F. Drucker said, "When you focus on strength, it puts a demand on performance." With elevated self-expectation, will come a new perspective on everything people do.

Questions to Ponder:
1. How would I describe my expectations of my team? How would my team describe my expectations?
2. Who is my most challenging person to work with? How might I adjust my perception/expectations of them?

Refine Your Execution

Routine Can Result In Reckless Execution

Elvin Bale was among the fourth generation of Bales in the circus industry. As a youngster, Elvin performed as a clown, a dancing boy, a cage boy for his father's tiger act, and an acrobat in the family's bicycle act. The circus was in his blood and there was no question that the circus would be his career.

Elvin was a tremendous trapeze artist by age seventeen. He concluded his trapeze act by sitting on the trapeze, swinging it up to its highest point, then diving forward into space with a yell —with no net underneath—throwing his legs back just in time to catch the middle of the bar on the descent with his Achilles' heels and swing back, hanging by his Achilles' heels. (I get goose bumps just visualizing this dare devil tactic).

Elvin was also known as "The Phantom of Balance" for his work on the "wheel of death". He mounted an 8-foot steel-mesh wheel on the end of a 38-foot steel arm suspended from the ceiling. As the arm spun around its axis, Elvin would run around the outside of the wheel, sometimes blindfolded, sometimes with a man standing on his shoulders. (Who's crazy enough to stand on his shoulders?)

In addition, he performed a high-wire motorcycle act, standing on his hands as much as 150 feet above the floor of the arena while riding the motorcycle backwards down the wire. Besides circus arenas, he also performed the motorcycle act on a high wire strung over a 300-foot canyon at Black's Beach near San Diego, California.

Elvin Bale has been called "the greatest circus daredevil of the second half of the twentieth century." In fact, Evil Knievel once shook his hand and told him he was crazy.

Elvin is perhaps best known now for his human cannonball act, which he began with Ringling Bros. and Barnum & Bailey Circus. in 1978 as the "Human Space Shuttle." This was by far the safest act in his repertoire. He was simply shot out of a cannon, flew through the air like a superhero, and landed on an airbag on the other end.

The circus cannon, despite the illusion and incredible noise it makes, is not a gun. It's all hydraulics and sound effects and functions like a gigantic piston. In preparation for each performance, sandbag dummies were used to calculate how much force was needed to project the flying human safely through the air and into the airbag on the other side of the big top. The dummy had to weigh exactly what Bale weighed to make accurate calibrations.

On the fateful day of January 8, 1987 something dramatic went wrong at the Hong Kong theme park. The sandbag dummy had been left outside on rain-soaked ground. Bale noticed the ground was wet, but the bag felt normal, so he didn't weigh before performing the test flight. Some of the sand inside was still wet making the dummy heavier than normal. The settings were calculated for the day's performance based on the weight of the dummy.

Bale had no clue anything was wrong until he was in mid-flight and realized he was flying faster and farther, then he was supposed to. Suddenly he was flying over the intended landing cushion.

Failure to EXECUTE was about to cost him dearly.

Bale recalled that he remained calm and thought through the adjustments he could make in his landing as everything seemed to be happening in slow motion. Maybe if he rotated his body, he could land on his feet rather than the normal back landing. He made the subtle adjustment just in time as he slammed feet first into the concrete floor shattering both ankles, a knee, a leg and his spine.

The world some had called the greatest daredevil was left paralyzed from the waist down at age forty-two.

Tom Peters was right: "The thing that keeps a business ahead of the competition is excellence in execution."

Routine Can Result In Reckless Execution.

_____

Questions to Ponder:
1. What things have we been doing so long we don't give them a second thought? Should we?
2. How can we refine our execution?

It's The Only Thing

Set An Enviable Standard For Those Who Follow.

I've learned it takes much less time energy and information to form an impression than to change one. Without naming names, think of all the public people who created a public impression they were unable to overcome and ultimately lost their impact and for some, their career.

Tony Campolo tells the story about a drunk who was miraculously converted at the Bowery mission. Prior to his conversion, Joe had gained the reputation of being a hopeless, dirty wino for whom there was no hope. But following his conversion to a new life with God, everything changed. Joe became the most caring person that anyone associated with the mission had ever known.

Joe spent his days and nights hanging out at the mission doing whatever needed to be done. There was never any task that was too lowly for Joe to take on. There was never anything that he was asked to do that he considered beneath him. Whether it was cleaning up the vomit left by some violently sick alcoholic or scrubbing the toilets after careless men left the men's room filthy, Joe did what was asked with a soft smile on his face and with a seeming gratitude for the chance to help. He could be counted on to feed feeble men who wandered into the mission off the street, and to undress and tuck into bed men who were too out of it to take care of themselves.

One evening, when the director of the mission was delivering his evening evangelistic message to the usual crowd of still and sullen men with drooped heads, there was one man who looked up, came down the aisle to the altar, and knelt to pray, crying out for God to help him change. The repentant drunk kept shouting, "Oh God! Make me like Joe! Make me like Joe! Make me like Joe!"

The director of the mission leaned over and said to the man, "Son, I think it would be better if you prayed, 'Make me like Jesus!'" The man looked up at the director with a quizzical expression on his face and asked, "Is he like Joe?"

When my actions are consistent with values and words are backed up with deeds, maybe I can become a "Joe."

One of the key components of leadership is to understand that your team will measure you by those consistencies (and inconsistencies). Simply, am I genuine?

John Maxwell reminds us that, "What people need is not a motto to say, but a model to see."

People are looking for someone they can believe in, have faith in, trust and support. I'm aware that if my team doesn't believe in me and what I represent, they won't believe in what I want to do or where I dream the organization can go.

Leaders, please set the enviable standard for those who follow you. Remember the wise council of Albert Schweitzer:

"Example is not the main thing in influencing others. It is the only thing."

Questions to Ponder:

1. What impression do you want to make on those you lead?
2. Do you spend more time overcoming an impression you've made than making the right impression?

"No Worse Than Anyone Else."

Avoid The Debilitating And Disabling Trap of Mediocrity.

Pulling no punches and telling it like it is; Tom Peters admonished a group of corporate executives to espouse a vision of excellence. He spoke to these leaders for several hours concerning product excellence, employee training, values, mission, and customer service.

Peters then opened the microphone for questions. Multiple attendees posed practical and philosophical questions on how to pursue 'excellence' in their company.

Unable to restrain himself any longer, an irritated executive interrupted Peters to voice his dissatisfaction with the message. "I'm sick and tired of hearing all this stuff on excellence," he blurted.

"Our company is no worse than anyone else!"

Wouldn't that be a great motto to hang over an organization's entrance or print on stationary: "We're no worse than anyone else." Now That's Vision!

I can't imagine receiving medical treatment, buying a car seat for a child, flying with an airline, or building a home with companies who claim to be no worse than anyone else.

Neil Armstrong, the first man to walk on the moon, was asked if he was nervous contemplating his trip into space. "Who wouldn't be," he responded. "There I was sitting on top of 9,999 parts and bits - each of which had been made by the lowest bidder!"

The Ministerial Association in a small community met to discuss the declining attendance in their churches. As the leaders discussed the predicament of their individual denominations, one pastor finally interjected, "It's good to hear the rest of you are having trouble as well. At least we're no worse than anyone else."

The "we're no worse than anyone else" attitude debilitates personal and organization excellence.

Those with the courage to rise above the current level of mediocrity will enjoy a distinct advantage. Their vision propels and compels them to new levels of performance. Lawrence Miller offered this sound advice; "The achievement of excellence can only occur if the organization promotes a culture of creative dissatisfaction."

I'm reminded of the story of the two back-packers who spotted a grizzly bear stalking them. One person calmly sits down, takes off her hiking boots, and puts on a pair of running shoes. "What good will that do?" asks her companion. "You can't outrun the grizzly." Lacing up her shoes, the friend responds, "I just have to stay ahead of you."

A commitment to be our best, creating a culture of creative dissatisfaction and taking corresponding action are the running shoes that keep us one step ahead of the "we're no worse than anyone else" crowd.

"Once you say you're going to settle for second," said John F. Kennedy, "that's what happens to you in life, I find."

Your mission (should you decide to accept it) is to create a compelling vision of excellence, sustain your commitment, hold tight to courage, and light a fire of passion that drives you to destroy the status quo. Envision a future, or a present for that matter, that paints a picture of who you are and where you want to be.

Questions to Ponder:

1. Where have we settled for the status quo?
2. How do we avoid the "we're no worse than anyone else" mentality?
3. What do you want to look like, feel like, and be like?

Perk Up Your Ears
You Ain't Learning If You Ain't Listening.

Long time talk show host Larry King shared this experienced piece of wisdom: "I remind myself every morning: Nothing I say this day will teach me anything. So, if I'm going to learn, I must do it by listening."

Listen! Listen! Listen!

Research indicates that most people speak at a rate of 150 to 200 words per minute, but the mind can process about 500 to 600 words a minute. That's why when I'm speaking to a group it always concerns me that they are probably already thinking about dinner that night and it's only mid-morning.

I've had to work hard at becoming a 'good' listener. I attempt to enter every conversation with a reminder to myself who the most important person is in this conversation. It's Not Me!

Former Chrysler Chairman Lee Iacocca advised, "A leader has to show curiosity. He has to listen to people outside the 'Yes, sir' crowd in his inner circle. The inability to listen," Iacocca continued, "is a form of arrogance. It means either you think you already know it all, or you just don't care."

That's what I would call a 'reality check.'

What's a leader to do?

Here are a few questions to stimulate a listening self-assessment:

Am I sincerely interested in other people's ideas? You can't fake this one. People can see (or at least judge) whether you are truly interested by your body language, facial expressions and attention. Be fully present. People won't speak the truth or share their heart if they feel the truth or their feelings don't matter.

Do I ask thought-provoking questions that allow people to speak their heart? Leadership expert Max DePree suggested "We do not grow by knowing all of the answers, but rather by living with the questions." Somebody once said, When I talk, I only know what I know. When I listen, I not only know what I know, but I also know what you know.

Do I intentionally get feedback to determine my team's position on potential ideas, opinions and projects? Pastor Robert Schuller once said, "Big egos have little ears." For the next '30' days don't make a permanent decision, take critical action, or pursue any new direction without first asking your team's opinion. Ask: "What do you think?" See how that feels.

Do I 'hear people out' without interruption, criticism or defensiveness? Enough said. You might be amazed at the number of fabulous ideas, innovations, opinions and great ideas that surface without non-judgmental feedback.

Finally, **what percent of the day do you spend 'telling?'** What percent do you spend 'listening?' I don't know the perfect percentage, but I'm not sure we can listen too much.

An investment in listening produces a great return...people feel valued, fresh ideas surface and the trust between the team and the leader is nurtured.

"The most basic of all human needs is the need to understand and be understood," suggested Ralph Nichols. "The best way to understand people is to listen to them."

Questions to Ponder:
1. What question(s) on the listening assessment struck a nerve with you?
2. What is your action plan?

Increase Your Bun Order

Decide Not To Participate In Doomsday Campaigns

A man made a comfortable living for several years selling hot dogs along the side of the road of a tourist community. He had difficulty hearing and his sight was deteriorating so he didn't read the newspaper or listen to the radio, but he was passionate about his hot dogs.

His sophisticated marketing was a hand painted sign declaring how good his hot dogs were. He enthusiastically announced to every passerby that they should buy his hot dogs...and they did.

He was obsessed with providing the best thick tasty hot dogs and warm buns possible for his customers. He passionately let his potential customers know what they would be missing if they passed up his hot dog stand.

The hot dog stand grew into quite a prosperous business. He increased his hot dog and bun orders and even purchased a larger grill to keep up with the demand. Then his eldest son came home from college and said, "Dad, what in the world are you doing? Haven't you been listening to the news? We are in the middle of an economic crisis. Europe is struggling. The Asian economy is teetering on failure. There's historic chaos in Washington, D.C. Tourism is in the tank. You could lose your healthcare and social security. What are you doing expanding your operation?"

The elderly man figured his college educated son must know what he is talking about. So, he took down his sign, decreased his bun and hot dog order and quit announcing to passerby's how delicious his hot dogs were.

Sales Plummeted!

"You're right," the old man said to his son a few weeks later. "We are certainly in the middle of a recession. Good thing you warned me."

DOOMSDAY is all around us. Decide not to participate.

Heed Patrick Lencioni's warning that, "If you're not willing to do things that others would say are over the top, and if you're not comfortable being criticized for being annoying and for having standards that seem perhaps just a little too high, then you'll drift toward mediocrity."

Mediocre Standards and Expectations Breed Mediocre Results.

Extraordinary Expectations Set the Stage for Extraordinary Results.

In other words...**Increase Your Bun Order.**

What's an unthinkable thing to do right now in your world but if you could pull it off, it would dramatically change the quality of what you do?

Willingly mess with worn out, worshipped processes, policies & procedures to pursue this one unthinkable thing. It will catapult you past doomsayer results.

Remember, what got you to where you are won't get you where we want to go...look beyond the tried and true and pursue the unthinkable.

Questions to Ponder:
1. What Doomsday prophecy have you bought into? How can you counterattack the impact?
2. What is that unthinkable thing?

Undercover Boss

Don't Wait To Go Undercover To Discover Reality!

Consider this provocative thought by James Stockdale: "When the crunch comes, people cling to those they know they can trust - those who are not detached; but involved."

Not detached...but involved.

When the television show Undercover Boss hit the airwaves, I was hooked. I was fascinated at the discoveries bosses made in this television reality show by going incognito. Religiously, I tuned in every week to see what profound discoveries the next boss would make about their organization. I must admit, I also enjoyed hearing the decisions bosses made to make life better in their companies.

I secretly and silently aspired to be one of those undercover bosses. Certainly, I couldn't mess things up any worse than the bosses I was watching on my flat screen. At the same time, I found the whole concept of going 'undercover' a bit troubling.

Why does the CEO need to become someone she isn't, to go to the frontline to find out how people really feel about the company? Why is he suddenly surprised to find out that some of the company's policies, processes and programs are anti-productive? Why does a boss have to go to sit in an employee break room to learn they have disgruntled team members? Why is there such a disconnect between corporate headquarters and the heart of productivity? For that matter, how can a direct supervisor be so unattached to what is happening around them every day?

I might suggest we all take inventory of how well we listen to people at the grassroots level; those who truly make things happen. They could no doubt save the company substantial time, money and effort if only we asked their input and advice. Undercover Boss caused me to reevaluate my understanding, listening quotient.

So, boss, if you were incognito, what do you think you would learn?

Forget the television show. Let me give you three questions to randomly ask your team members. You will discover boundless information that will help you improve effectiveness, engagement, and efficiency without going undercover.

The answers to these three questions are worth the price of an expensive, elite education.

Questions to Ponder:
1. What one thing could I do that would improve the quality of your life?
2. What one frustration, if I could eliminate it, would make your work life easier?
3. What can I do to help you become the best at what you do?

People and Profits

The Hard Stuff Results From Paying Attention To the Soft Stuff.

Entrepreneur Marcus Lemonis declared, "I believe in people, process and product, but people are the most important thing."

A dynamic work environment cannot be announced, proclaimed or manipulated. We can't mandate it. We can't legislate it. It grows out of our deeply held beliefs about people. It flows out of the hearts and minds of leadership.

"Spirit does not need to be 'brought into' an organization," wrote Marie Morgan. "Spirit already lies within virtually every employee. It is waiting to be released and provided with a hospitable and nurturing environment—policies, structures and systems, behaviors, norms, and habits to support what people prefer. A place to work that feeds their spirit and produces a fine and worthy product or service."

For you leaders who find this culture stuff too "soft," the plain truth is, until you pay attention to soft stuff—culture, you're not going to get the hard stuff—dollars.

Consider this. The U.S. Department of Labor compared seventy-five companies that use traditional "command and control" philosophy with seventy-five "progressive organizations," that is, those with programs for worker involvement, training, teamwork, and profit sharing (the soft stuff). Over five years the traditional companies showed an average annual increase in profits of 2.6 percent. The progressive companies showed a 10.8 percent increase.

"I used to believe that culture was 'soft,' and had little bearing on our bottom line. What I believe today is that our culture has everything to do with our bottom line, now and into the future."
Vern Dosch, Wired Differently

Companies that are focused on building culture generally grow faster, increase revenues and improve their bottom line.

Thomas Watson, the former IBM CEO recognized the importance of culture. He once commented: "Our early emphasis on human relations was not motivated by altruism, but by the simple belief that if we respected our people and helped them respect themselves the company would make the most profit."

A study conducted by Deloitte Consulting tracked the shareholder returns of the 56 publicly traded firms on Fortune magazine's 100 Best Companies to Work For list in 2006. The facts revealed that those companies consistently outperformed the S&P 500.

Robert Levering, author of A Great Place to Work, said, "What's important about a great workplace is that profits are not something to be achieved at the expense of the people responsible for creating them. A great workplace suggests that it's possible to achieve that success while enriching the lives of the people who work there."

Creating culture is plain old good business.

I am reminded of a bit of verse created by Milliken & Company that reads,

The hard stuff is easy
The soft stuff is hard.
And the soft stuff is a lot more important
Than the hard stuff.

Think about it.

_____

Questions to Ponder:
1. Do my strengths lean toward taking care of the hard stuff or soft stuff?
2. If the people stuff precedes the profit, how will I adjust?
3. What actions can we take to create a better balance?

Unblemished Excellence

Impressive, jaw-dropping, incredible results rarely grow out of marginal expectations

---

John Ortberg suggested that, "We are called to be perfect, not be perfectionists. Perfect is unblemished excellence. Perfectionism is moral obsessive compulsive disorder."

Lou Holtz believes that "to strive for perfection means you've got to be totally dedicated. It can't be an occasional thing - it's got to be a total dedication in everything you do. If you don't have total dedication to perfection in your life, then I believe your attitude toward life is flawed."

As a coach, Lou Holtz fervently imbedded that attitude in his players. In his book *Wins, Losses, and Lessons*, Holtz reflects on his experience at Notre Dame. He told his players from the outset that, "less than perfection is a personal embarrassment to me, to you, and to this university."

I often wonder why we are so fearful today of the word 'perfection?' Is it the mystery, the impossibility of achieving or the fact we've eliminated it from our vocabulary, so no one feels overwhelmed or defeated with such high standards?

Leaders who consistently preach and live the message that less than 'unblemished excellence' is inconsistent with who we are and the path we are traveling, inspire the team to perform with heightened focus and purpose.

A little irrational exuberance can be just the fuel needed to light an inspirational fire.

I contend it begins with expectations. Impressive, jaw-dropping, incredible results rarely grow out of marginal expectations. I have found that weak expectations produce mediocre standards followed by lackluster effort producing unspectacular results. On the flip side, high expectations plus energetic planning plus brilliant execution equals wonderful world class outcomes.

Make good enough, excusing mistakes or justifying lackluster effort a thing of the past. Dismantle those mindsets at all costs. Beware of lowering your standards to pamper people who are satisfied with mediocrity. Those are not the people who will make your team great. Appeal to those people who want to be the best and are willing to pay the price to pursue unblemished excellence.

I understand people who question this fanatic pursuit of success - unless they are on my team. Their dispassionate attitude has the capacity to squelch any potential mountain top achievement.

Believe in the people who will help you achieve peak performance. Be there to help them be the best person they can be and the best team member possible. Never allow your team to settle for less than they can contribute. When people do their best to give their best they will feel the best about themselves.

Leaders who take their teams to new heights continually raise the bar for their team's performance. Think about the specific ways you can set the tone to nurture an organizational culture that consistently exceeds expectations.

Remember the wise words of Coach John Wooden:

"Perfection is impossible, but we must constantly strive for less imperfection."

So now, if this strategy doesn't result in 'unblemished excellence' it will certainly catapult you so far ahead of the average team that the chasm between you and them will be incredible.

Some of you might be thinking this is a preposterous notion. Don't go there...

You might be on the verge of achieving something incredible with unblemished excellence.

Questions to Ponder:
1. Are there results we've 'settled for'? How do we raise the expectation?
2. What does 'less imperfection' mean in your world?

Out of the Weeds

Don't Major In The Minors Or Minor In The Majors.

I love Aesop's fables! Their simple messages often teach us powerful lessons.

Remember "The Fox and the Cat?" A fox boasted to a cat one day about how crafty and cunning he was. "I've got all kinds of tricks," the fox said. "For example, whenever I hear dogs coming, I know a hundred different ways to escape."

The cat was impressed and modestly replied, "Your cleverness is amazing. As for me, I have only one way to escape, and that is to climb up a tree. I know it's not as exciting as all your ways, but it works for me. Maybe someday you could show me some of your different escape routes."

The fox smiled smugly, "Well, friend, perhaps I'll have some free time one of these days, and I can show you a trick or two."

Shortly afterward, the fox and the cat heard a pack of hounds nearby. "They're coming this way!" The cat shrieked. She quickly scaled a nearby tree and hid herself in the leaves.

The fox stood there trying to decide which of his many tricks to use. Paralyzed with indecision, the fox waited too long to make his move, and the hounds pounced on him.

Team members can be paralyzed by too many priorities, projects or plans, complicated by unclear expectations.

Ask your team to make a list of all the initiatives and projects they are currently involved with. Once the list is finished, ask them to cross through any that are not important.

I can predict with a high rate of success that very few items on the list are eliminated. Someone, in some way finds them important.

Often teams become overwhelmed by 'doing' all the important things without necessarily achieving outstanding results. Or, even worse, everything seems important, so people don't know where to start. They are so caught up in the weeds of self-imposed (and other imposed) demands that their effectiveness is being impacted and their efficiency is minimized.

The cat knew the one thing that kept her safe and secured her survival. How about taking a similar approach with your team?

Have each person consider this question: **"What one thing can you accomplish in the next week (month, year) that will have the greatest impact on your success?"**

Now, ask team members to dedicate their best energy to that one thing. Once accomplished, refocus on a new 'one thing,' accomplish, and move on.

Leaders, run interference for your team by helping them eliminate the minor things that drain energy and get in the way of results.

Remember the words of Johann Wolfgang von Goethe; "Things that matter most must never be at the mercy of things that matter least."

Questions to Ponder:
1. What is your biggest drain on energy?
2. When do you feel paralyzed?
3. What is the one thing you can accomplish in the next week (month, year) that will have the greatest impact on your success?

Achieving Olympic Performance

Break The Monotonous Mold Of Mediocrity.
Embrace The Excellence Expectation.

Like it or not, J. Willard Marriott was right; "All organizations are perfectly designed to get the results that they get."

Peter Vidmar, former Olympic gymnast, shared with an audience the difference between an Olympic champion and an Olympic gymnast. To achieve a perfect 10 in gymnastics, according to Mr. Vidmar, involves three additional factors; risk, originality, and virtuosity. Each of these elements can add .2 points to a great score of 9.4, driving the total to a perfect 10.

To become a world class champion requires scoring on elements worth measuring.

What a wonderful analogy for any business. There is a distinct difference between just doing what we do and becoming an 'Olympic

Champion' organization. The ongoing aspiration and challenge is to position ourselves in such a way that we achieve the highest level of results possible.

If we're intent on becoming a business Olympian but the journey seems to be filled with curves, roadblocks and detours, then it might be time to rethink the route we're taking.

Maybe you work and work and work but the results remain the same. Successful organizations don't just ride it out hoping the results improve. They get serious, push harder, experiment with alternative approaches and quit doing the things that fail to produce the desired results. In other words, they make sure the systems, processes, and procedures that are in place...really work - and modify or eliminate those that don't.

When you're not achieving your lofty standards; don't lower the standard, refine the process. Peter Senge calls the difference between where we are and where we want to be Creative Tension. Creative Tension can serve as the accelerator for invigorated, new, fresh strategies that are required for a break-through performance.

You can't attain champion status by becoming 'more' ordinary or predictable. Seek remarkable. Whether intentional or accidental, break the monotonous mold of mediocrity by embracing an Olympic performance mindset.

Get through the current barriers, failures or dead ends and you'll discover success on the other side. Current challenges and set backs are simply an invitation for you to do something exceptional.

Being old(er), I've endured a number of life enriching set-backs. So, I'm also keenly aware how easy it is to get into the rationalization, blaming, 'excusiology,' or justification mode of thinking. We become experts at defending our less than exceptional results and explaining how it's the best we can expect under current circumstances.

Don't go there.

Never give up on or explain away something with fabulous potential because your current condition feels overpowering. If it's worth investing in, forge ahead with courage and unwavering determination.

Today, your Olympic performance pursuit is either stalled, slipping backwards or gaining forward momentum. Don't settle for mediocre because you're too busy to invest in World Class. Schedule the priorities into your calendar that really matter. Get focused.

You have to raise the level of expectation to raise the level of performance. John Maxwell believes, "It's not about meeting expectations; it's about raising the standard."

You and your team have the power to determine the ultimate outcome.

Questions to Ponder:

1. Where do your results stand? Where do you want to be? What is the gap? Who needs to be involved to determine how we get there?
2. What is the one thing you can do to dramatically impact your world class results? What are the elements that can drive your score to a perfect '10?'

Create Opportunities for Success

Enable People To Do Uncommon Things.

Our local newspaper printed an interesting article entitled "All Work, No Feasting: Cormorants are Chinese Fisherman's Friends."

The Chinese fisherman sets out in his row boat with four to six sleek, oily-feathered, foxily fast cormorant birds. Thin lengths of twine in a ring are placed around the cormorant's necks. The nooses ensure that try as they might the birds are unable to swallow the fish (except the very small ones).

The birds and the men find a promising spot and everyone is set to go to work. The cackling cormorants are released to do their work. The birds swim around the boat looking for their prey and then in flash make a dive and catch the fish in its beak. The ring prevents the larger fish from being swallowed. The fisherman allows the bird to eat the little fish that slip through the ring but the larger fish are the fisherman's to keep. The cormorant quickly dives again for another catch.

Over and over the cormorant dives, catches a fish, surfaces, has the fish taken from its mouth, and goes back into the water to repeat the process. Their industriousness and precise fishing skills make the well-trained cormorants extremely valuable to the Chinese fisherman.

How many skilled, well trained team members set out to do their best every day and are rewarded with only the smallest catch? The 'big fish' (fun, significant, priority stuff) are reserved for the leader to enjoy while the 'little successes' provide a token reinforcement to keep people satisfied.

Avoid 'dumpagating' or 'relegating' undesirable tasks, projects or miniscule assignments. Take the ring off people's necks and allow them to experience the big catch. Leaders create the opportunity for people to perform at the highest level.

Keep in mind; you cannot be responsible for people's success. However, the leader is responsible to people. The responsibility for success (or failure, for that matter) lies within each person. But, leaders create the conditions for people to succeed...or at least improve the opportunity to succeed.

Years ago, Peter Drucker declared, "The purpose of an organization is to enable common men to do uncommon things." His thought is as pertinent today as it was then. Creating opportunities for success is not about the things you do to and for people. It's removing the barriers, impediments and obstacles that currently restrict success.

Allow people to spread their wings, take some risks and experience the incredible satisfaction of seeing their efforts result in significant accomplishments.

Questions to Ponder:

1. What undesirable tasks have I dumped lately?
2. How can I increase the opportunities for people to experience personal success?

Implement Operation Appreciation

Complimentary People Are Complimented By Those They Complement With A Heightened Desire To Earn The Compliment They Received.

I'm convinced that no one, regardless of position, power or education, is immune from the desire for respect and recognition. Insightful leaders are keenly aware that appreciation and encouragement are oxygen to the soul.

In fact, Psychologist William James discovered, "The deepest craving of human nature is the need to feel appreciated."

My experience has been that appreciated people will always do more than they are expected to do.

A man walks into a greenhouse and watches an employee work with a group of plants. The longer he observed he noted a strange scenario. There was one plant that was receiving no water, nourishment or attention. The bystander couldn't resist satisfying his curiosity by asking, "Sir, could you tell me why you're watering and fertilizing all these plants except that one.

The gardener held up the plant and responded, "You mean this one?"

"Yes, tell me why?"

"This plant," replied the gardener, "really, ought to want to grow."

Ridiculous, right? Yet that silly example exemplifies the leader who has decided people ought to want to grow without her encouragement and attention. People want to make a difference. They want to feel significant.

Be an opportunist. Look for simple unsuspecting, spontaneous, heartfelt ways to reveal and recognize people's importance.

I'm old enough to remember the leadership style that believed if people do something wrong, point it out in vivid detail. When they do something right, leave them alone. You certainly wouldn't want to interrupt a good thing. (I might have even bought into that concept in my early days).

People ought to want to do a great job with or without being appreciated. That level of thinking is archaic and constipates people's potential. Even worse, how many number "10" performances go unnoticed, unrecognized and unrepeated because a leader didn't take time to celebrate it?

Complimentary people are complimented by those they complement with a heightened desire to earn the compliment they received.

Wal-Mart founder Sam Walton said, "Outstanding leaders go out of the way to boost the self-esteem of the personnel. If people believe in themselves, it's amazing what they can accomplish." Mr. Walton made self-esteem boosting a way of life. It was just good 'people business.'

Appreciation is one of the leader's most powerful simple tools for catapulting people to higher levels of performance and therefore infuses their lives with natural self-esteem boosters. A simple word of recognition from someone who believes in us is life enriching, if not life changing.

If operation appreciation hasn't been a part of your leadership repertoire, do whatever it takes to implement it now! You certainly don't want your team to suffer from ADD (Appreciation Deficit Disorder).

Questions to Ponder:

1. How do I go about individually recognizing each person on my team for their contributions

Unleash the Imagination and Power of Your Team

Never Underestimate the Powerful, Practical Wisdom of Your Team.

I'll never be content with having a team of people who just show up and do what they are asked to do. I want people who want to be here. They want to contribute. They want to give their best. They are passionate to make a difference in people's lives. They aspire to reach for new heights of excellence. They believe in what they do. They want the best for the company. And, I've learned my job is to inspire (sometimes gently push) them to a higher level of performance than just coming to work.

A participative environment is a natural extension of a leader's belief in people's potential. Leaders intent on identifying and developing people's strengths weave throughout the culture opportunities to influence decisions. A participative leadership style is an expression of my heartfelt desire to see people grow, contribute and be fulfilled.

It's important to note that participative cultures are not dictated, policy driven or protected by bureaucratic layers that stymie people. People come to us with various packages of abilities. To unleash these gifts to be expressed and expanded in different ways allows the formation of a culture where people can touch greatness. Isn't that what leadership is all about—making a significant difference in the lives of those we are privileged to lead.

Creating a participative environment is about respecting people enough to show them that success isn't possible without their engagement and involvement. This simple, yet profound, realization will not only inspire heightened performance but will bolster self confidence and nurture loyalty.

As Dan J. Sander wrote; "Cultures focused on people unleash the imagination and lift performance to new heights - to a higher purpose."

Walk Around. Not the "I'm checking up on you" walk around. I'm talking the "how can I support and learn from you walking around."

There's a monumental difference. One is precipitated by the need to control. The other is driven by a desire to encourage others to take ownership.

See Something. Say Something. "I like the way you just handled that challenge." "Thank you for the way you just treated that customer." "Your positive attitude is definitely showing - thank you." "Great idea! Try it."

Ask Advice. What do you think? How can we improve? Any ideas how we can get 10% better? Is there a better way? What advice do you have before I decide? How have you learned to improve this process? Simple questions. Powerful message.

Priority. What is the most important thing you are working on right now? What seems to dominate your time? What are you hoping the result will be? What can I do to help you make that happen?

Never underestimate the powerful, practical wisdom of your team.

When we realize, we don't have all the answers, when we ask for people's opinions, when we create a safe place for ideas to be shared, when we reach out to secure several perspectives, we communicate the respect we have for people.

Involvement breeds commitment and commitment breeds a spirit of ownership and responsibility.

Then, impressive things get done.

Questions to Ponder:

1. Am I willing to share leadership with my team? How will I make that happen?

Who Pushed Me In?

Foster An Environment Of Faith Not Fear To Fervently Foster Faithful Followership.

Tom Peters rightly observed: "It's horrifying how easy it is to demotivate someone. To dent/diminish/destroy their fragile psychological ownership of a task!"

One of the quickest ways a leader can demotivate or drain the energy of a team member is to employ fear as a 'motivational' tactic.

Ted Engstrom, writing in *Motivation to Last a Lifetime* tells about a party being held on a cruise ship. Speeches were being made by the captain to the crew and guests enjoying the week-long voyage. Sitting at the head table was a seventy year old man who, somewhat embarrassed, was doing his best to accept the praise being poured on him.

Earlier that morning a young woman had apparently fallen overboard, and within seconds this elderly gentleman was in the cold, dark waters at her side. The woman was rescued, and the elderly man became an instant hero.

When the time finally came for the brave passenger to take the podium, the entire room fell into a hush as he rose from his chair. He went to the microphone and in what was probably the shortest "hero's" speech ever offered, spoke these stirring words: "I just want to know one thing - who pushed me in?"

Cute!

Major message: People working in a world of fear and control feel "pushed into" most everything they do.

In our world of wonderful advances, I marvel at leaders who endorse this archaic approach with people. It seems that such a discussion should be unnecessary. Yet, there are leaders who have not yet realized that fear motivation restricts, inhibits, freezes and stresses. It causes panic, tension, hostility, bitterness and anger. What few results that are achieved are short lived and lack the commitment to follow through.

A sign posted on a ranch fence in Western South Dakota epitomizes my point. The sign reads, "Don't attempt to cross this field unless you can do it in 9.9 seconds. The meanest, ugliest, nastiest bull in South Dakota can do it in 10 flat!"

People who step into the ring with a fear inducing leader feel they are continually running for their life.

Leaders who emulate the behavior of a mean nasty bull will always have people on the run—away from them. Leaders choosing fear to 'motivate' people to action; get ready to lose the faith, confidence and respect of those around you.

Create an environment of love—truly caring about people—and watch people blossom.

P.S. This message applies to parents as well.

Questions to Ponder:
1. Are my actions motivated by love or inducing fear?
2. What behaviors might I display that cause fear to surface in people?
3. Who fears me the most? How can I turn that fear into trust?

Prove It!

You Can't Fatten A Cow By Weighing It!

President Adams made this observation: "Facts are stubborn things; and whatever may be our wishes our inclinations, or the dictates of our passions, they cannot alter the state of facts and evidence."

Isn't that the truth!

President Abraham Lincoln provided the perfect example. He was attempting to make a profound point to his Cabinet members. He posed this question:

"If you took a calf and called the calf's tail a leg, how many legs would the calf now have?"

Several members of the Cabinet suggested, "Five."

At this, Lincoln pointed out, "No, the calf still has only four legs. Calling a tail a leg does not make a tail a leg."

The moral of the story is quite apparent. Dreaming, declaring, or hoping a fact is true has little significance or impact on whether it is.

Most of us possess something called confirmation bias— I learned that in my college freshman psychology class. This bias says we see what we are looking for, hear what we want to hear and look for information that confirms what we believe.

Thus, confirmation bias.

More importantly, we tend to filter out what doesn't support our bias. Be honest. We've all done it.

The prudent move is not to manipulate what I experience to fit my bias but to apply the reality of my experience to eliminate my bias. In short, I need to separate facts from fantasies and ensure that my perceived results reflect reality.

It's not as complicated as it sounds.

George Bernard Shaw reflected: "The only man who behaved sensibly was my tailor; he took my measurement anew every time he saw me, while all the rest went on with their old measurements and expected them to fit me."

Like the tailor, we need to continually measure our performance so we're not making decisions, touting our achievements or moving into the future using outdated measurements. Even more important, is what we're measuring moving us in the direction of our ultimate goal?

What is your competitive advantage? What sets you apart from everyone else in your profession? What makes you superior to those around you? Can you deliver on the promise no one else in your profession is willing to make?

Prove it!

Declaring it doesn't make it so.

Jessamine West asserted, "We want the facts to fit the preconceptions. When they don't, it is easier to ignore the facts than to change the preconceptions."

Isn't that the truth!

A fundamental key to business success is understanding your competitive advantage and being able to "prove it" with anecdotal and quantifiable results.

Demonstrate it. Let your actions and results be consistent with your declarations.

Repeat it. Consistently.

Questions to Ponder:
1. What do you aspire to become?
2. What data do you have to prove you are on your way?

Problems. Policies. Principles.

People Don't Respond Progressively Better When Being Treated Progressively Worse.

I'm not naive. I know there are two or three problem people in the world and they find their way into every organization. When you are blessed with their arrival, and their problem performance raises its ugly head, you have one intelligent, proactive, courageous action to take: go straight to the person and work to resolve the issue.

Open, honest, dignified, straightforward communication promotes a problem-solving attitude. Developing a new policy just irritates those who are already living the mission and values of the company. Rules should never be used as a substitute for making solid decisions and confronting people about things they should or shouldn't be doing.

As Duke Basketball Coach Mike Krzyzewski puts it, "The truth is that many people set rules to keep from making decisions."

Think about this little mind twister. Do your people produce policies or do policies drive your people? Policies need to be written to keep people in line—right? People who mess up need to be punished. This reminds me of the criminal justice system I once worked in (which is a more appropriate place for this mentality). A dynamic work environment builds personal commitment and responsibility by holding people accountable for their performance. Punishment gets us neither.

With few exceptions, people don't respond progressively better when they are treated progressively worse through petty, pedantic, punishing policies. A 'get by' mindset settles in and people merely avoid getting caught or take their medicine and consider the score equal. People aren't searching for more rules to live by but a purpose they can believe in and live.

When we handle people as individuals, with trust and respect, the majority will respond in kind. So, what about the small percentages that won't? As Warren Bennis suggested, "Don't overreact to the grumblers and trouble makers." They should be invited to work for a competitor. Free up their future. Encourage them to seek their happiness somewhere else.

Our goal is not punishment. It's problem-solving. Encouraging productive behavior. Improving performance. The heart of the message is to treat people equitably, not equally. Policies often attempt to treat everyone the same. As John Maxwell says, "Managers wrestle with the 'fairness issue.' Leader's don't." Why? Leaders are naturally 'fair-minded.' Managers search for equality.

If you want to lift people to a higher level, create policies for the majority, not the minority. "Nothing short-circuits good people and great service," believed Mary Kay Ash, "than 'company policy.'" Policies are the ultimate expression of company bureaucracy. Principles, on the other hand, establish the expectations.

Thank you, John Maxwell, for providing this thought provoker: **"Policies are many. Principles are few. Policies will change. Principles never do."** Let principles guide your tough people decisions. They stand the test of time. Never be bashful about using your principles to set a standard for people to attain and sustain.

Questions to Ponder:
1. How well do people understand the principles that guide our team?
2. Are there policies in place that inhibit acting on principles?
3. Is our team dependent on principles or policies to guide their actions?

If You Want People To Be What You Are Then Become What You Want Them to Be.

Be Who You Want Others To Be.

───────────

Ghandi suggested, "Be the change you want to see in the world."

It is impossible to establish a culture with a policy manual or set of operating procedures. The leader's behavior is the single most important factor in demonstrating to their team what behaviors are expected. The culture is set by what leaders do and who they are.

Before you ever utter a word in the morning, the team has already assessed your mood and anticipated behavior. How you walk in the door, your facial expressions, and the look in your eyes confirms the attitude they sense when you say, "good morning."

Your willingness to pitch in to help do the menial tasks, the events you attend, your response to problems, and on and on and on—they all impact the intensity people feel about the organization's values.

I love the comparison of thermometer and thermostat leadership. There is a dramatic difference! The thermometer is a very practical tool that allows us to know what the temperature is. Its purpose is to report the current data. The thermostat gives us control of that data. Adjusting the thermostat allows us to adjust the comfort level.

Thermometer leaders have a finely tuned sense of what the culture is but that's it. They are frustrated, elated, concerned, confused or pumped by what they 'feel' as they walk the halls, introduce new ideas, participate in meetings and establish performance expectations. Thermometer leadership is popular. Ineffective—but popular.

Thermostat leaders are culture setters. They understand that how they come to work will determine the temperature for the day. Culture is dramatically influenced by their behavior and they know it.

Thermostat leaders learned long ago the prevailing presence of the "One-Upmanship" game. If leaders decide to be crabby, down in the mouth, or have a lousy attitude; they quickly learn that their team members can one-up them without much effort.

Face it, leaders are not allowed to have a bad day. If you are having a bad day, no one should know about it. During challenging times, a leader's primary challenge is to refrain from feeling sorry for themselves, getting down, expressing anger or allowing people to see a diminished spirit.

Somebody once said 90% of the people don't care about your problems and the other 10% are glad you have them. Don't wear it on your sleeve. Suck it up. Work through it but don't get your team wrapped up in the details of your difficulties. A demotivating, problem focused, whining leader will undoubtedly create a corresponding culture.

Mentally shred gossip, rumors and complaints about others.

Maintaining this confidentiality speaks volumes about the way you expect your team to treat each other as well as other departments.

In high school biology, we injected red dye into a potato. To our amazement every inch of the potato showed red in the veins. A leader's action, attitude or perception is injected into the organizational culture and life source of every team member. They will become us.

"People look at you and me to see what they are supposed to be," said Walt Disney. "And, if we don't disappoint them, maybe, just maybe, they won't disappoint us."

Questions to Ponder:
1. What do I expect others to be? What behaviors are expected? How do I model that behavior?
2. Do I reflect the qualities of a thermometer leader or a thermostat leader? What actions can I take to infuse the culture with new energy?

How Do You Want Me to Treat Others?

Treat every person you encounter as the most important person in your life.

———————

Ralph Waldo Emerson suggested if you treat people greatly they will show themselves great.

One of the benefits people focused leaders experience is that because of the way they live and treat people, others are interested to hear what they say...in that order. Nothing is more confusing than to hear a powerful sermon about how important people are and then be treated like second class citizens.

How a leader treats others is one of the most important factors in demonstrating what they 'really' believe in and stand for. Care, truly care, about people. Go to the wall for your people. Stand behind people to support and gently nudge them along then, go in front of them (if needed). Listen. Cheerlead. Hug. Be the kind of leader that people know they can depend on to be emotionally consistent.

Don't throw them under the bus. Don't make people your scapegoat. Don't ever treat someone in a way that strips their dignity. Don't criticize in public. Don't be caustic...or sarcastic. Don't devalue people in anyway.

Buck Rodgers reminds us that, "Respect for others is the bedrock of all relationships, even the most casual, and must be demonstrated whenever we have the opportunity. In a business situation, it's an imperative."

I'm reminded of the elderly gentleman being tailgated by a high-strung woman on a busy city street. Suddenly the light turned yellow just in front of him. Being an ex-driver's education instructor, he did the right thing, stopping for the yellow even though he could have beaten the red light by accelerating through the intersection.

The tailgating woman lost her cool, laid on the horn, went into a verbal rampage hanging her head out the window to display her disgust. As she was still in mid-rant a finger gently touched her shoulder and she looked up into the eyes of a very serious police officer.

The officer kindly asked her to exit her car with her hands up. He took her to the police station where she was searched, fingerprinted, photographed, and placed in a cell. The raving driver was now a quiet prisoner.

A few hours passed before a jailer made his way back to the cell and opened the door. She was escorted back into the booking area where the arresting police officer was waiting with her personal belongings. He said, "I'm very sorry for this misunderstanding. You see, I was following you down the street when the light turned yellow. When you began blowing your horn, ranting and raving, and cussing at the gentleman, I got confused. I noticed the 'What Would Jesus Do?' bumper sticker, the chrome plated Christian fish emblem on your trunk and 'Love One Another' license plate frame."

"Naturally, I assumed you had stolen the car."

Treating everyone as the most important person in your life doesn't sound that difficult until we add this caveat – all the time whether you want to or not.

Everyone! All the time!

Questions to Ponder:
1. How do I elevate people's view of themselves?
2. How does my treatment of others exhibit what I preach?
3. Would I like others to copy the way I treat people?

Stupid Mistake...Let's Have Lunch

Eradicate The Fear Of Failure Complex.

College roommates spent a quiet Friday night watching an old classic western. As the cowboy galloped along on his horse, Paul bet his roommate $10 the cowboy was going to ride over the cliff.

"No way," he said. "The bet is on."

Sure enough, moments later the horse rider disappeared over the cliff. Paul collected the $10 but then started feeling guilty. "I can't take your money," I told him, "I've seen the movie before."

"So, have I," the roommate responded. "I just didn't think he would do it again."

Promoting learning and allowing for mistakes doesn't mean I allow people to repeat the same silly mistakes repeatedly getting the same mediocre or even fatal results.

Peter Senge was right; "People are designed to learn. Organizations are designed to control." Controlling environments don't respond well to mistakes. Controlling leaders point fingers. "Who" not "What" failed dominates an unhealthy leadership mentality.

Immediately. Right now. Eliminate all signs of the "mistakes are bad" mentality. Eradicate the fear of failure complex. Remove the stigma attached to making blunders and bloopers. Rather, make them a vital part of your learning environment.

Charles Knight believes, "You need the ability to fail. I'm amazed," he said, "at the number of organizations that set up an environment where they do not permit their people to be wrong. You cannot innovate unless you are willing to accept some mistakes."

I have a little sign in my office that says, "Stupid Mistake. Let's Have Lunch."

That's my philosophy in dealing with mess-ups. I can handle any unintentional failure or mistake. But there must be a plan to make this a learning experience that ensures the same mistake doesn't occur again.

Risk takers, willing to be fully accountable for their efforts, are powerful arsenal for any team. It is important that team members sense a "go for it" spirit and confident level of support. Leadership encouragement is the fuel that ignites their productivity.

It's unfortunate, but people are often waiting for the leader's permission to try their "next best thing" idea to avoid the potential of failure embarrassment.

"Bottom line (According to Tom Peters): Mistakes are not the "spice" of life. Mistakes are life. Mistakes are not to be tolerated. They are to be encouraged. (And, mostly, the bigger the better.)"

———————

Questions to Ponder:
1. What is my reaction to failure and mistakes?
2. How can I use people's strike outs as learning experiences?

Look Beyond the Obvious

Clarity Of Vision Translates Into Urgency And Execution.

Burt Nanus declared, "There is no more powerful engine driving an organization toward excellence and long-range success than an attractive, worthwhile, achievable vision for the future, widely shared." I've come to realize that visionary (forward-looking) leadership is not a nicety—it is a necessity. Today's effective leaders foresee the need for change and are willing to empower people to prepare for and address it. Under this leadership, organizations remain on the cutting edge of progress.

"Vision is not so much what you think as how you think," wrote Peter Koestenbaum in *LEADERSHIP: The Inner Side of Greatness*. "Vision," he said, "is less a matter of content than process. Vision is moving away from micromanagement, from 'flyspeck management' to macro leadership."

I like that!

Meeting the challenges of today's fast-paced, ever-changing world requires leaders to re-evaluate their readiness to address the needs of the future. Facilitating change, creating vision and empowering people are primary tools in a leader's progressive repertoire. Leroy Eims, author of **Be the Leader You Were Meant to Be**, suggested that, "A leader is one who sees more than others see, who sees farther than others see, and who sees before others do."

Roberto Goizueta, the former Chairman of Coca-Cola, was a visionary. The story is told that one day he asked a question of his senior managers:

"What is our market share?"

"45%," came the proud, confident reply.

"How many ounces of liquid does a human being need to drink a day?" Goizueta asked.

"64 ounces a day," came the quizzical reply.

"On average, how many ounces of all of our products does a person drink per day?" Goizueta asked.

"2 ounces," someone quickly replied.

"What's our market share?" came his final question.

Startled by this stretching thought, the senior managers suddenly realized the soft drink market wasn't saturated and substantial potential for growth still existed.

Goizueta's vision altered the direction of this well-established traditional thinking company. By rattling people's thinking and expanding their vision, the competition was no longer the other soft drink companies. The quest became growth opportunities around the world by competing with any other beverage.

Robert Goizueta believed, "If think you are going to be successful running your business in the next ten years the way you did the last ten years, you're out of your mind. In order to succeed, we have to disturb the present."

To disturb the present, I need to give people a clear picture of how the vision will impact the future and then watch them rattle the status quo and create something special.

Without a clear vision, people are easily distracted. Clarity will translate into urgency and execution.

Questions to Ponder:
1. What is my concrete, stretching vision for the future?
2. How can we 'disturb the present' to produce the desired future?

A Code To Live By

Make What You Believe Come To Life In Words, Actions & Attitudes.

_____

During my college years, Crosby, Stills & Nash released a hit song about ethics with the line: "You, who are on the road, must have a code that you can live by." Every person and company can benefit from a 'code' that guides their daily behaviors.

Tom Peters and Robert Waterman put it this way: "Let us suppose that we were asked for one all-purpose bit of advice for management, one truth that we were able to distill from the excellent companies', research. We might be tempted to reply, 'figure out your value system.' "

'Figure it out.' Are your values becoming solidly engraved into the company culture?

Every action I take as a leader loudly declares my level of commitment to the values. As a leader, you can gauge the effectiveness of your day by the consistency of your actions with your stated values.

Living our values sets us apart! Values tell the world who we are by the way we act, provide services and treat one another. Countless companies proudly display their values on banners and websites, but their actual behavior is inconsistent with who they say they are.

Walt Disney was a master at setting Disney productions apart from all the rest and making the customer experience consistent with the values. Disney is in business to provide an intangible product called happiness. Their "Disney Courtesy" concept is based on four key values - safety, courtesy, show and efficiency. Every performance standard is measured by these deeply held beliefs and they are expected to be incorporated into the lifestyle of every cast member.

Disney cast members are indoctrinated with the philosophy and standards of "guest service." No cast member begins their role without substantial orientation to Walt Disney's vision of service. Employees think, walk, talk and breathe safety, courtesy, show and efficiency. It is a way of life. This lifestyle creates happiness for guests.

Values are those closely held beliefs you support with your thoughts, words, feelings, and actions. Your values describe the desired conduct expected of every team member. The "feeling" inside your team reflects how closely the values and behavior are matched.

The Tomb of the Unknown Soldier in Arlington National Cemetery in Washington, D.C., has a guard 24 hours a day. Every thirty minutes, 365 days a year, a new soldier reports for duty. When the new guard arrives, he receives his orders from the one who is leaving. The words are always the same:

"Orders Remain Unchanged."

Just like those orders, your "code to live by" remains consistent, immovable, non-negotiable, and unchanged. Carefully ponder each phrase inside your values.

I concur with Max DePree. "A corporation's values are its life's blood," he said. "Without effective communication, actively practiced, without the art of scrutiny, those values will disappear in a sea of trivial memos and impertinent reports."

Questions to Ponder:
1. Are our values a 'way of life' on our team?
2. What current attitudes, actions and performance have I observed that reinforce the values?
3. What adjustments do I need to make?
4. Where do I need to raise my expectations of others?

Building High Performance People

People Are Assets Worthy Of Your Investment.

Years ago, I sat mesmerized watching a 60 Minutes segment in which Mike Wallace was interviewing one of the Sherpa guides from Nepal who helps climbers reach the top of Mount Everest.

"Why do you do it?" Wallace asked.

"To help others do something they cannot do on their own," answered the guide.

"But there are so many risks, so many dangers," said Wallace. "Why do you insist on taking people to the top of the mountain?"

The guide smiled and said, "It's obvious that you've never been to the top."

Taking people to the top is unimaginable unless you're on the journey yourself.

Powerful leadership is not about me—what I want, what makes me feel good, what makes me comfortable or what makes me get ahead. It's about my desire and ability to help transform people's lives. It's about taking people to new levels of performance. Taking them to the top of the mountain.

Bill Gates suggested: "Empowering leadership means bringing out the energy and capabilities people have and getting them to work together in a way they wouldn't do otherwise."

People know when an organization believes in them. People know when their leader wants to take them to new heights. People know when someone wants to help them become a better person. People know when teams are created to cooperatively achieve uncommon results. These are ultimate compliments.

Empowerment tends to be a much used, over used, abused, misused term to describe everything from giving people the freedom to do what they want to do to making it possible for people to do what they've never done.

I view empowerment as building high performance people. It includes expanding opportunities for people to turn potential into achievement and accept full responsibility for results. Empowerment isn't something I do to people. Rather, I create a culture that is conducive for people to produce superior results and take accountability for those results.

W. Steven Brown writing in *13 Fatal Errors Managers Make* says, "A manager should never become more concerned about his or her people's success or failure than they are. The responsibility for their success or failure lies with them, not with the manager. Learn this lesson: you cannot be responsible for people. However, by necessity, you must be responsive to people."

I find that to be a challenging and worthwhile balancing act. When I am responsive to people they will be more responsible and achieve new performance heights.

People are a valuable, appreciating asset only if we are willing to invest in them.

Questions to Ponder:

1. How do I feel about the arduous, exciting task of taking people to the top?
2. What characteristics inside our work culture make it possible for people to ascend to new levels of performance? What barriers need to be removed?
3. How am I continually ascending to new levels so I can guide people to new levels of achievement?

Three Keys to Influencing People

You Will Never Move Ahead Until Your Team Is Behind You.

Ken Blanchard touched the heart of leadership effectiveness when he said, "The key to successful leadership is influence, not authority."

Leaders interested in influencing their team, need to understand how their actions impact people. Leaders may get compliance by exerting their authority but genuinely influencing people is a whole different matter. Here are '3' factors I've observed in influential leaders.

Likeability

"Leadership must be likeable, affable, cordial, and above all emotional. The fashion of authoritarian leadership is gone."
—Vicente del Bosque

"Likable" is defined by Mr. Webster as, "having qualities that bring about a favorable regard."

Dr. Sheldon Cooper, PhD, genius theoretical physicist and dysfunctional social character on the television sitcom **The Big Bang Theory** epitomizes the opposite of the likeable character Webster describes.

Although endearing as a comedy television character, Sheldon's OCD personality combined with his lack of relational skills serve as a continual irritant to those around him. He's blatantly direct without any clue of how insulting his approach can be. Sheldon's lack of emotional sensitivity results in frequent hurtful comments and behavior that prompts unfavorable regard.

His friends and fellow intellectuals 'endure' him but are repeatedly embarrassed by and the target of his arrogant, discourteous, pointed behavioral tendencies.

I must say he plays the character impeccably well. But, his lack of relational and personally appealing skills will never win him a spot in the "likability hall of fame."

Some people are just naturally likable. People gravitate toward them. When they enter a room there's a certain comfort that permeates the space. I envy those people.

On the opposite end of the continuum are those who draw smiles and relief when they leave a room.

Although mystical, maybe we make being likable too difficult. Norman Vincent Peale was right. He said, "Getting people to like you is only the other side of liking them."

This question may sound strange. Are you likable? Do you like others?

It seems to me (I know this sounds simplistic) that we should desire to be likable and mold our leadership style around being a likable person. For some reason that doesn't sound profound, but it is.

Here are a few strange but valuable self-assessment questions: If I worked for me would I like me? Am I the type of person I would enjoy being around? Am I naturally pleasant? Do I have friendly facial expressions? Does my non-verbal behavior communicate warmth?

Likable people are naturally friendly, personable, engaging and interested in people's lives. Of course, cool, disagreeable or emotionally disconnected people normally don't fall into the 'likable' category. Likable people genuinely like people and people know it.

Being likable doesn't guarantee people will follow you. Conversely, being unlikable will virtually guarantee people won't voluntarily follow you. Besides, being likable will make it easier and more pleasurable for people to interact with you.

People like people who are likable. Rarely do we spend extensive time with people who are unlikable. Thus, it is virtually impossible for us to build trusting, fruitful, productive relationships if we are unlikable.

Likability opens the door for people to feel comfortable approaching us, engaging in conversation or allowing us to lead, coach or mentor them. In addition, if people like you they tend to give you the benefit of the doubt and are willing to listen to your message. Without it, there is a disconnect.

Clarification; likability is not the same as trying to make everyone happy. Not even close. Likable leaders will still need to make decisions, communicate messages or implement plans that not everyone is going to like. Likability is not the result of making everyone happy but genuinely acting in people's best interest.

Remember Michael Scott from the television series The Office? Here's his perspective: "Do I need to be liked? Absolutely not. I like to be liked. I enjoy being liked. But it's not like this compulsive need to be liked. Like my need to be praised."

Next is:

Transparency

Transparency is removing the mask and revealing the real you.

Leaders can suffer from feedback deficit and a diluted self-assessment. It's true—it is easy for me to become out of touch with the truth about me. It's more common than you would imagine. In fact, the higher up the ladder a leader climbs, the less accurate the self-assessment is likely to be. Why is that? Because the higher the position the less likely people are to give honest feedback.

Hans Christian Andersen's The Emperor's New Clothes is a classic parable with a relevant application for leaders. A vain Emperor who is obsessed with wearing and displaying elegant clothes hires a couple of swindling weavers to make him a new suit. These characters convince the Emperor they are using a special material that is invisible to those who are stupid, incompetent or unfit for their positions.

The Emperor parades before his subjects fitted in his new 'suit.' The townsfolk play along with the scam, not wanting to appear stupid or unfit for their positions. Then a child in the crowd, too young to understand the peer pressure to keep up the facade, blurts out, "But he isn't wearing anything at all!"

Transparency equals vulnerability. Ironically, a lack of transparency multiplies your vulnerability and minimizes your authenticity.

You may want to read that again.

Transparent leaders allow people to see the 'real' you. The emperor's obsession to have the perfect public persona backfires. Only the little boy was honest enough to 'expose' the absurdity of the Emperor's persona. Sharing your heart with people confirms what they think about you or reveals the challenge they have balancing what they see with what they hear.

Transparency ultimately says; "what you see is what you get." Sincerity. Genuineness. The Real You. Are you the same person at work as you are at church, the ballgame or shopping in your local grocery store? Is there a connection between what you profess and what you live?

Transparency communicates the message to hold me accountable to be who I say I will be and do what I say I will do.

Transparent leaders naturally attract followers through their genuine, integrity laced, open persona. As Janet Louise Stephenson suggested, "Authenticity requires a certain measure of vulnerability, transparency, and integrity."

Finally,

Vulnerability

**"In the beginning, people think vulnerability will make you weak, but it does the opposite. It shows you're strong enough to care."
–Victoria Pratt**

In the 1992 movie A Few Good Men, Colonel Nathan R. Jessep (played by Jack Nicholson) is called to the witness stand. Lieutenant Kaffee, a young, aggressive attorney played by Tom Cruise, is drilling the Colonel.

Kaffee is grilling Jessep with tough, digging questions. Jessep finally loses his patience, and temper, and in a violently heated manner he blasts Kaffee: "You want answers?"

Kaffee snaps back with equal emotion, "I want the truth!"

Jessep snaps, "You can't handle the truth!"

The truth makes us vulnerable. Along with vulnerability comes the twin—authenticity.

Authenticity—knowing who you really are and knowing the truth about yourself as viewed by others. Someone once said; the truth about you is you don't even know the truth about you.

I must admit, that thought frightens me at times.

Starbucks founder Howard Schultz suggested, "The hardest thing about being a leader is demonstrating or showing vulnerability. When the leader demonstrates vulnerability and sensibility and brings people together, the team wins."

Leaders work under the illusion that they know how they are perceived in the organization and yet, I fear most of us are clueless to the real perception that exists. Ironically, most leaders prefer not to receive feedback that would reveal their team's predominant impression of their leadership.

Self-Reflection and Evaluation are the first steps to greater awareness and authenticity. How comfortable are you with your history—your life to this point? Are you willing to openly share your failures, challenges, successes and struggles? Can people see how you have arrived at this point in your life? How well have you accepted everything that has brought you to where you are?

Coach K (Mike Krzyzewski) observed; "People are not going to follow you as a leader unless you show them that you're real. They are not going to believe you unless they trust you. And they are not going to trust you unless you always tell them the truth and admit when you were wrong."

I submit that great leaders make it a point to identify their own mistakes, flaws and weaknesses and openly admit them to their followers. It makes us human. Admitting my shortcomings is also a proactive approach to reality rather than letting others define my weaknesses. Own you for who you really are.

Authenticity, the truth about you, begins with coming to amicable terms with your past and using it to teach others and prepare yourself (and them) for the future. Overcome the temptation to pretend to be someone you're not. Keep it real. Charles Swindoll exclaimed: "I know of nothing more valuable, when it comes to the all-important virtue of authenticity, than simply being who you are."

Then, can I handle the truth about how others see me? How big is the gap between what I think and what others think? The bigger the gap, the more frustration I create. Am I comfortable hearing from others about my effectiveness or ineffectiveness as a leader? What am I doing that works or doesn't work?

Brene Brown was right. "When you stop caring what people think, you lose your capacity for connection. When you're defined by it, you lose your capacity for vulnerability."

Get comfortable in your skin and understand how others see your complexion.

Closing thought:

French Author Andre Malraux asserted, "The first duty of a leader is to make himself be loved without courting love. To be loved without 'playing up' to anyone – even to himself."

There is no right way, nor is there only one way to influence people. There are countless factors that contribute to the level of influence leader's experience.

Leaders may get compliance by exerting their authority or positional power but genuinely influencing people requires a whole different attitude and skill set.

Christian Herter, former governor of Massachusetts, learned during his second campaign that position doesn't automatically give you influence. One day Herter arrived at a church barbeque after a long day of campaigning with minimal food. As he walked through the serving line, he held out his plate to the woman serving chicken. She smiled, put one piece on his plate and turned to the next person in line.

"Excuse me," the governor said. "Would you mind if I have another piece of chicken?" "Sorry," said the server. "I'm only supposed to give one piece of chicken per person." "But I'm famished," Governor Herter responded. Still smiling, the woman responded, "Sorry, only one per customer."

The governor was a nice, mannerly, and humble man but he was also incredibly hungry. He decided to use his position to influence the lady. "Mam, do you know who I am?" he said. "I am the governor of this great state."

"Do you know who I am?" the woman responded. "I'm the lady in charge of the chicken. One piece per person. Now, move along."

Position rarely achieves long-term influence, impact or results. Relationships, on the other hand, are a leader's asset and fast track to influencing others.

One thing is sure...**You will never get ahead until your people are behind you.** How?

I've concluded my role as a leader is not to control people or stay on top of things, but rather to encourage, energize, and excite.

Activating that belief requires a leader to shift from a policy, micromanaging, control mentality to a people driven, relationship building, inspiring mentality. People notice the difference and the difference will have a notable impact.

Striving to be a likeable, transparent and vulnerable leader is an honorable pursuit that ultimately produces substantial doses of influence and inspiration. Likeability, Transparency and Vulnerability—the triplets of influence.

Questions to Ponder:

1. What makes you likable? Less than likable?
2. How might the Emperor's behavior be compared to a leader's situation?
3. What is your personal reaction to the thought that, the truth about you is you don't even know the truth about you?
4. Do people respond more to my position or my people skills?
5. Who is the last person I inspired to pursue new heights by my leadership?

Stepping Into The Future

People Must Be Willing To Give Up 'What Is' to Experience 'What Could Be.'

I am inspired by words of James M. Kouzes & Barry Z. Posner; "Leaders are pioneers. They are people who venture into unexplored territory. They guide us to new and often unfamiliar destinations. People who take the lead are the foot soldiers in the campaigns for change...The unique reason for having leaders - their differentiating function - is to move forward. Leaders get us someplace."

Remember the words of King Solomon as written in the book of Proverbs, "Where there is no vision, the people perish." Sometimes, even a vision isn't enough.

God sent Moses to deliver the Israelites from captivity in Egypt. Now Moses wasn't excited about the idea but agreed, with God's help, to lead His people into the Promised Land. A well-orchestrated escape plan worked beautifully and as the people approached the Promised

Land, spies were sent ahead to check out the situation. One man from each of the twelve tribes was chosen to represent them on the scouting excursion.

The Israelites anxiously awaited their return and report. The scouting summary prompted chaos. Ten spies saw giants who would crush them like helpless grasshoppers. Jacob and Caleb, on the other hand, saw a land "flowing with milk and honey." "Let's do it," they encouraged. "You're crazy," said the others. The majority won and because of their fear, the people died in the wilderness - except two. Joshua and Caleb entered the Promised Land.

God had already promised the Israelites safe entry. Yet, with a guaranteed vision clearly before them, the Israelites chose to follow their self-imposed limitations. How Sad! Such opportunities are also overlooked today because leaders lack the faith and determination to pursue a vision - and they are slowly perishing.

"One essential ingredient for being an original in the day of copies is courageous vision," declared Charles Swindoll. As you envision the ideal future for your organization, be ready to endure criticism, skepticism, and downright humiliation. Not everyone loves leaders who are attempting to create something special.

People must be willing to give up 'what is' to experience 'what could be.'

But oh, how difficult it can be to move from the comfort of where I am into the unknown—especially if there are perceived hazards.

The Israelites were guaranteed success but when a few people became fearful of what 'could be,' the majority hung on to what they had—and perished.

Before we can build a great future or great teams or organizations, we need to vividly imagine them and believe beyond a shadow of a doubt that our vision is achievable.

Every day in some small or flagrant way, people face individuals or groups who oppose any thought that challenges their present world. One noticeable quality of visionaries is their refusal to listen to the short-sighted doomsayers who could only see as far as the first obstacle.

Max DuPree, legendary former chairman of Herman Miller and author of the influential book *Leadership Is an Art*, offers great advice to leaders: "When it comes to vision and value, you have to say it over and over and over again until people get it right, right, right!"

Questions to Ponder:

1. How can I regroup the troops and get them headed toward the desired future?
2. Who are the team members most likely to help us get there? How can I encourage them?
3. Do I have team members who might sabotage our move into the future? What position will I take with them?

Just Sit Right Back...

Look For The Sunshine In Every Cloudy Experience

Facebook Executive Jennifer Dulski sees it this way, "The key to success is holding on to the belief that you'll have more sunny days than cloudy ones and to just keep climbing, every day, no matter what. Great leaders not only keep climbing on both types of days but also inspire their teams to climb with them."

"Just sit right back
And you'll hear a tale
A tale of a fateful trip,
That started from this tropic port,
Aboard this tiny ship.
The mate was a mighty sailin' lad,
The Skipper brave and sure,
Five passengers set sail that day,
For a three-hour tour,

A three-hour tour..."

I predict 80% of you acquainted with television from 1964-1967 (or reruns) have the tune from the television show Gilligan's Island rattling through your brain.

Even if you don't, never fear, this message is still for you.

On Gilligan's Island, the passengers on board the S.S. Minnow's three-hour tour found themselves in survival mode on a remote, uninhabited island after encountering an unexpected storm in their tiny ship.

Every episode focused on a highly diverse group of people (sound like your team?) learning to coexist, cooperate to overcome adversity and deal with Gilligan's bubbling, often outrageous efforts to get off the island (and you thought you were the only team with a Gilligan).

Regardless of the situation, one character remained calm, positive and realistically optimistic in every episode. The Skipper. He found the 'sunshine' in cloudy circumstances. The Skipper's positive attitude and engaging smile kept the castaways calm even in their most desperate situations.

The Skipper supported every potential effort, possibility or devised solution to get off the island. He was fabulous at finding the positive in every solution and never belittled people's desperate ideas to return to civilization.

The Skipper possessed the incredible leadership ability to exhibit a fresh approach every morning to a nagging old problem—how to get off the island. He kept hope alive, recognized the positives in every situation and never allowed circumstances to dampen his spirits.

Who would have thought a silly 1960's sitcom could be loaded with leadership lessons?

As leaders, we are called to enliven people's spirits, see the possibilities and provide hope when circumstances are grim. Michael Hyatt reminds us that, "You've got to decide as a leader that one of your primary roles is to be inspirational."

If you need a little help, Google the theme song to Gilligan's Island and enjoy a little retro inspiration...(I'm headed over there now...)

———————

Questions to Ponder:
1. Does my team see me as an instigator of energy, optimism, creativity and/or positivity?
2. How can I bring "calm" in difficult situations?
3. Who could I encourage to pursue their "bumbling" ideas?

Prepare People to Fly

Help People Achieve Heights Previously Not Imaginable.

Peter Drucker had incredible insight into the life of a leader. This observation is especially inspirational: "Leadership is not magnetic personality - that can just as well be a glib tongue. It is not making friends and influencing people—that is flattery. Leadership is lifting a person's vision to high sights, the raising of a person's performance to a higher standard, the building of a personality beyond its normal limitations."

Denis Waitley, writing in *Empires of the Mind*, reminds us that eagles could easily teach leadership to the less focused human species.

When it's time to lay her eggs, the female eagle locates a perch high on a mountain, selects suitable materials, and assiduously prepares the nest. She works carefully and very hard, following mental blueprints of great functional quality. After the eaglets are born, she spends virtually all her time responding to their needs. She hunts for fish and small game to ensure that they are properly nourished—which is an eaglet's sole task, apart from sleeping and crying for more food.

Instinct tells the eagle that the day will soon come when her offspring must make their own way. Somehow, she knows that feeding her eaglets will be followed by a second, critical task of teaching them to fly.

When she senses the eaglets are ready, she puts them on alert by stirring up the nest. One morning, she returns from an outing without food. Moving to the edge of the nest, she uses her sharp beak to rip out big chunks, and then drops them from the cliff. As the chunks fall hundreds or thousands of feet to the canyon floor, the eaglets watch and look at each other in astonishment. The eagle continues for several hours ripping apart the sturdy nest she built with such care and skill. What had given the eaglet's total security is now a most uncomfortable resting place.

After stirring the nest, the eagle begins fluttering over her brood like a helicopter. Then, while the eaglets watch intently, she sits on the nest and thrusts her beak into the air. When a breeze blows up from the valley, ruffling her feathers, she balances herself until the wind begins to gust. Then the perfect role model hurls herself into it. Catching the front end of the breeze, she hovers above the eaglets. No other bird can do this: The hollow bones that enable eagles to fly higher than any other bird also allows them to hover. Meanwhile the eaglets, if not yet graduates in aerodynamics, learn that the wind is their helper for controlling flight.

Repeating her demonstration several times, the eagle flies to a vantage point out of the eaglet's sight. They hesitate a moment, some more than others. And then they begin to fly.

It's quite the process to get the eaglet from birth to independence. The mother eagle's intuition, nurturing instinct, training regimen and her ability to let go serve as an incredible example for every leader intent on preparing their people to fly.

Leaders are continually nurturing, coaching and mentoring people to fly to greater heights. A primary characteristic of dynamic leaders is that they are fiercely obsessed with helping people be successful. They understand that along with the privilege of being a leader comes the responsibility to be a servant and thus commit themselves to their team's growth and success.

Questions to Ponder:

1. How am I nourishing and nurturing my team members to achieve greater heights?

What's Your Aim?

If You Don't Think It, You Can't Achieve It

Tom Peters admonished companies to, "Aim for 'insanely great' or don't bother."

The Steinway piano has been the keyboard of choice by such masters as Rachmaninoff, Horowitz, Cliburn, Litszt and many others. And, for good reason. The Steinway is universally accepted as a skillfully crafted instrument that produces extraordinary musical sound.

Steinway pianos are built today the same way they were built over 150 years ago when Henry Steinway initiated his meticulous approach to building a phenomenal musical instrument. Catch this...200 craftsmen and 12,000 parts are required to produce one of these magnificent instruments.

The manufacturing process includes rim-bending, where 18 layers of maple are bent around an iron press to create the shape of a Steinway grand. In addition five coats of lacquer are applied and hand-rubbed to give the piano its outer finish and glow.

The instrument then goes to the Pounder Room, where each key is tested 10,000 times to ensure lasting quality and durability.

This handcrafted instrument is manufactured to display the talents of the most gifted keyboard masters.

Insanely great threatens those who prefer 'what is' and excites the 'Steinways' of the world.

I see an incredible gap between leaders who settle for minimal immediate satisfaction and those in pursuit of long-term optimal gratification by aiming for 'insanely great.'

Trying our best to become extraordinary often results in the conclusion that it's just too overwhelming, stressful and demanding. That's like saying exercise is too exhausting.

Of course, it is!

If I am passionate about achieving insanely great results, I've got to be willing to pay the price. The pursuit of insanely great requires us to do what is difficult to achieve because we know it is right.

The work you do is determined by how big you think. You don't do big until you think big. You can't become insanely great unless you think insanely great.

Questions to Ponder:
1. "What do we need to do/stop doing to get from where we are to where we need to be?"
2. Are we doing different things that move us toward Insanely Great?
3. What's your next step toward insanely great?

A little about the old guy...

Glenn Van Ekeren is the President of Vetter Health Services in Omaha, Nebraska, a company committed to providing "dignity in life" for the elderly. He is a frequent speaker on leadership and principles for maximizing people and organizational potential.

He is the author of a number of books including **12 Simple Secrets to Happiness, Speaker's Sourcebook I and II, Love is a Verb** and is a featured author in several **Chicken Soup** books.

For more of Glenn's wit, humor, and inspiration, follow Glenn's blog on enthusedaboutlife.com.

Made in the USA
Monee, IL
07 March 2021